DATABASES

How to manage information on your micro

PETER LAURIE
Southdata Ltd

Designed by Bernard Higton

CHAPMAN AND HALL/METHUEN
London New York

First published in 1985 by
Chapman and Hall Ltd/Methuen London Ltd
11 New Fetter Lane, London EC49 4EE

Published in the USA by
Chapman and Hall/Methuen Inc
733 Third Avenue, New York NY 10017

Diagrams by Trevor Bounford
Illustrations by Val Hill

Printed in Great Britain at the
University Press, Cambridge

ISBN 0 412 26380 7

Laurie, Peter
    Databases: how to manage information on your micro.
    1. Data base management   2. Microcomputers
    I. Title
    001.64'42   QA76.9.D3
    ISBN 0-412-26380-7 Pbk

Library of Congress Cataloging in Publication Data

Laurie, Peter.
    Databases : how to manage information to your micro.

    Bibliography: p.
    Includes index.
    1. Data base management.   2. Microcomputers
Programming.   I. Title.
QA76.9.D3L38   1985   001.64'2   84-22976
ISBN 0-412-26380-7 (pbk.)

CONTENTS

	Preface	
1	**The computer**	
	1.1 The introspective typewriter	9
	1.2 Disks and data	11
	1.3 The operating system	14
	1.4 Peripherals	16
	1.5 Mice versus finger tips	22
	1.6 Multi-user micros	26
	1.7 Virtual memory	28
	1.8 How computers communicate	29
	1.9 The latest in data storage	31
	1.10 Bugs	35
	1.11 The cost of software	37
	1.12 Crashes and backups	37
2	**What is a database manager?**	
	2.1 The intelligent filing cabinet	40
	2.2 Indexing	45
	2.3 Hashing	47
	2.4 Serial indexes	50
	2.5 B-tree indexes	51
	2.6 To sort or not to sort	57
3	**Using a database manager**	
	3.1 Forms (and filling them in)	59
	3.2 Computer security	63
	3.3 Speedy answers	64
	3.4 Searching the databases	66
	3.5 Deleting records	70
	3.6 Reports	70
	3.7 Programming around the database	72
	3.8 Text databases	73
	3.9 Picture databases	76
	3.10 Spread sheet packages	77
	3.11 Graphics	79

4   **Multi-file databases**

4.1   Relational calculus   87
4.2   Hierarchical databases   93
4.3   Windows   95
4.4   The problem of updating data   97

5   **Enquiry languages**

5.1   Programming languages   100
5.2   Programming in Superfile   102
5.3   A visual approach   106
5.4   Schemes and data dictionaries   109
5.5   Prolog   109

6   **Data: sources and costs**

6.1   Distributing data   115
6.2   Computerizing all sorts of data   118
6.3   Accuracy   121
6.4   Data protection laws   123
6.5   The obsolescence of history   124

7   **The intelligent database**

7.1   The problems of information   132

References   135

Index   136

PREFACE

This book is an introduction to the basic ideas of database management. This may seem an unnecessarily esoteric subject until one reflects that very few offices, and indeed very few homes, do not contain a card index or a filing cabinet, and that if the information they contain were transferred to a computer it would be – by definition – a database. If one believes that within five years every office worker will have a personal microcomputer, then the corollary is inescapable: we shall all have to understand database management.

Amateurs in the computing field should find this a challenging but rewarding book. Because of the huge market for microcomputers and the equally huge lack of knowledge about them, there is a vast premium at the moment on 'user-friendly' software which purports to work without any help from the user. The current crop of easy-to-use database software often does not, in my view, address the real issues in information management. There is great pressure to invest programming effort in gimmicks that will make the naive and potential purchaser of the equipment believe that he or she does not have to understand how the machine works. To change the analogy somewhat, today's micros are rather like the motor cars of 1910. You *could* drive to Peking (or Beijing) in them, but you had to be prepared to regrind the cylinder block by hand somewhere back of Lhasa. If you went motoring you soon became a competent mechanic. By the same token, if you are not computerate when you begin a database project, you certainly will be by the time you bring it to a happy conclusion. As Kutuzov, the Russian general who opposed Napoleon's invasion, used to tell the chaps, 'Train hard, fight easy.'

Professionals in the computing field may find this an intriguing but rather unorthodox book. Until recently, database management has been an important but small and remote speciality. Few people worked in it and they have developed a theory of database management at a high level of abstract discussion. At times the theory seems almost ritual in its opacity and irrelevance to what appear to me to be the real needs of users. When, in 1980, I needed to find out about this subject because my company was starting to write and publish a database package*, I found surprisingly little that was useful in the existing texts.

We wrote the software by the light of nature – and very lucky we did too (see Chapter 4). My knowledge of what databases ought to do started from

---

*The package is called *Superfile* in the UK and Europe, *Avatar* in the US; the company Southdata Ltd.

talking over the last three years to some thousands of people who wanted to manage information on micros. These conversations led to endless debates with the programmers – headed by my son Bennet, without whom there would be no Southdata, no Superfile and no book. By dint of a lot of talking, arm-waving, programming and trying the results out on real, live customers we slowly arrived at what seems to us to be a workable product. Out of it too has come this book which will, I hope, illuminate some puzzling corners of an important subject.

I must apologize in advance for letting my own business preoccupations intrude into the argument. An author is supposed to be impartial; to have no commercial axe to grind. Unfortunately the world of computing is so young and so small and expanding so rapidly that anyone with any ideas is expressing them in as many ways as possible. It is like the Wild West: the sheriff who prosecutes you for cattle rustling often turns out to own the largest ranch in the territory. It is unfortunate but there are no innocent bystanders in computing either.

It would have been nice if this book could have served as a catalogue of currently available products, with their features described and an assessment of performance given. Unfortunately there are now just too many database packages; at least 60 are available in the UK alone and in the US there are more than 150 competing database software packages. To review a piece of software properly requires about a month's work, so the current offerings would take more than 17 years, by which time it will all be irrelevant.

This book is not intended as a handbook for software professionals. A glance at the 'bible' – Donald Knuth's *The Art of Computer Programming*, (1973), in seven volumes – will explain why no book this size could convey anything useful. The aim of this work is to outline the salient issues and techniques to the intelligent amateur, and still partly perplexed professional so that he or she stands some chance of picking a way through the jungle of competitive products.

CHAPTER ONE

THE COMPUTER

A database is a bunch of information held in a computer's memory. It is useful because one can look for things in it not just by the file number or the addressee's name, as with a paper filing system, but by almost anything that is in it. But before we talk about the trials and tribulations – and also the convenience and uses – of database management, it would be a good idea to digress here to talk about the salient features of the computer itself as it affects the user of a database system.

1.1 The introspective typewriter

One can – and many writers have – become quite philosophical about computers. For the present purpose, that is in considering how they can be used for the storage and retrieval of information in databases, a computer is just an electric typewriter (with a certain amount of introspection) built into a filing cabinet. By introspection I mean that you can ask the typewriter to look at what it has typed – not only recently, but two years ago – and ask it to, 'find me someone called "Tom" or anyone who owes me £500'.

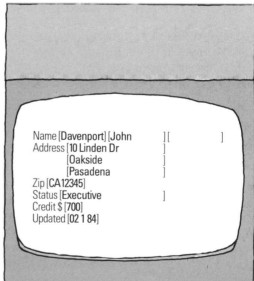

A 'Record' in a computer database (right) is much the same as the information one might write on an index card (left). Each item of information on the card goes into a labelled 'field' on the computer screen.

Information in a database is assumed (for the moment, but see Chapter 4) to consist of numbers of similarly shaped chunks of data. Each chunk is called a 'record'. A record is made up of 'items' which, in turn consist of 'fields' and 'values'. A field is a space for a particular type of information – a surname or the date a letter was written or the price paid for an object. A letter in a filing cabinet can be broken down into these components and would make a very suitable record in a free-text database. We will look more closely in later chapters at the way such things are organized.

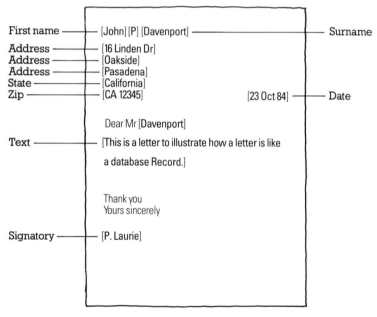

First name —— [John] [P] [Davenport] —————— Surname
Address —— [16 Linden Dr]
Address —— [Oakside]
Address —— [Pasadena]
State —— [California]
Zip —— [CA 12345]   [23 Oct 84] —— Date

Dear Mr [Davenport]

Text —— [This is a letter to illustrate how a letter is like

a database Record.]

Thank you
Yours sincerely

Signatory —— [P. Laurie]

The elements of a business letter can easily be seen as fields in a database Record.

A database consists of a lot of chunks of similar data held on a disk. Database management is all about memory and so, what the computer has to offer in this department is very important. The machine has two sorts of memory: its internal Random Access Memory (RAM) which is connected directly to the processor and its 'external' disk memory. External is in quotation marks because, although the disks may be built into the same box as the computer, they are logically and functionally exterior to it in the same way that the keyboard and screen are.

The RAM available in desk-top micros is relatively small – between 64K*

---

*1K = 1024 bytes. A byte is the unit of information storage and holds one letter or number.

and 500K. When the power is turned off the contents of RAM generally disappear. The disk holds data permanently (one hopes) and is much bigger. In modern desk-top micros you would expect to have about 1MB (million bytes) on a floppy disk and up to 20MB on hard disk. If you want to spend the money you can have many thousands of megabytes of disk storage. And, as we shall see later, devices are coming soon which will provide these huge storage capacities using cheap, new technologies.

One reckons that a text word is on average six characters long, so 1MB holds 166 666 words or about three ordinary sized novels. A good typist will rattle the keys at 80 words per minute – it would take him or her 33 non-stop hours to fill up a megabyte. But it is surprising how quickly even as much space as this disappears. The machine on which I wrote this has 16MB of disk and 15MB of it was full by the end. We could always erase the files that do not seem to be relevant, but, as sure as God takes bytes out of little green magnetic apples, that file will be the pride of someone's eye. It seems that most of the expensive hard disks in the world are three quarters full of files that no one can remember a thing about. A variant of Parkinson's Law – data expands to fill the storage available – applies very strongly. The new high capacity disks promise enough storage to hold a lifetime's work from a fast typist, which means they will take only a year to fill up.

The computer cannot do anything directly with data on disk. It has to be copied into RAM before it can be searched or arithmetic can be done on it. RAM is rather like your desk top; the disk is like the filing cabinet. You get selected papers out of the filing cabinet, work at them on your desk and put them back. However, if you are using a computer with a database manager, you have the assistance of a very fast and intelligent clerk who will find the papers you want from pretty vague hints about what it is in them.

1.2 Disks and Data

Data is stored on a disk – whether floppy or hard – as minute patches of magnetism. The patches go north to south to record a '1', or south to north to record a '0'. (Actually, as always, it is more complicated than that, but this is the general idea.) The 0s and 1s are called 'bits'.

The patches of magnetism are written into the magnetic material that covers the disk by the 'read-write' head. This is a tiny electro-magnet that skims the surface of the disk. Apart from the fact that it and the magnetic material both move, the principle is just the same as in a tape recorder where the head stands still and the magnetic material alone moves past it.

The same head† serves both to write new patches of magnetism and to

---

†There may actually be several heads and several disks or 'platters', but the principle is the same.

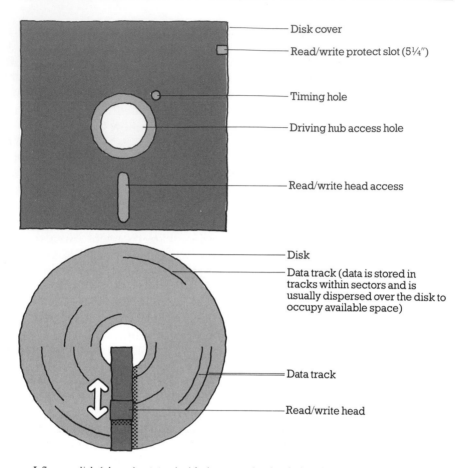

Disk cover

Read/write protect slot (5¼")

Timing hole

Driving hub access hole

Read/write head access

Disk

Data track (data is stored in tracks within sectors and is usually dispersed over the disk to occupy available space)

Data track

Read/write head

A floppy disk (above) rotates inside its cover (top) to bring data written on it under the read-write head. A hard or 'Winchester' disk works the same way except that the disk surface cannot be removed from the machine.

read old ones. The disk spins round and the head moves in and out so that every part of the disk surface can come under the head by a combination of these two movements. The head writes data in a series of concentric 'tracks' which are broken up into 'sectors'.

The operation that takes the time is positioning the head over the right track on the disk and waiting for the right sector to come round. This takes roughly a fifth of a second on a reasonable floppy disk machine. A hard disk takes about 1/300 of a second, but it has to swim its head about over much more data so the rate at which it can search in bits per second is perhaps only ten times higher. In estimating the amount of time that a database manager will take to do anything, you have to look at the number of disk accesses involved.

As must be well known in the western world by now, the bits represented by the little patches of magnetism of the disk are made up into 'bytes'. Each byte consists of eight bits; 1s or 0s. Since each bit can have two values – 0 or 1 – a byte can have $2^8 = 256$ different values, which is plenty for upper and lower case letters, numbers, punctuation, brackets and all the other characters one finds on a keyboard, plus some more.

A file consists of a string of bytes. What else could it be? The computer can interpret these bytes in several ways: as a command to its processor which means the file is a program; as letters and numbers, or in many other ways. Since databases are about human-type information, we want to look at the byte as a letter or a number – i.e. as the equivalent of a key on a computer keyboard. The generally used code is the American Standard Code for Information Interchange (ASCII) which assigns a number from 0 to 127 to each keyboard character. Upper and lower case letters have distinct codes and are treated as different characters. 'A' is ASCII 65, 'a' is 97. There are some 'non-printing' characters like Line Feed, Carriage Return etc. along with 32 invisible characters made by pressing the Control key with a letter. These are used by some packages to allow the user to give commands. In a word processor, for instance, Control F might mean move the cursor forward one character.

ASCII (as its name implies) is fine for Americans, but imposes a very annoying kind of cultural colonialism on its users. The difficulty arises from the representation of language-specific characters like é in Spanish or ç in French. ASCII assigns codes to these letters but it assumes that a user wants either Spanish or French but never both at once. Thus, for instance, ASCII code 43 is the hash sign in America or the pound in Britain but not both. If, in Britain you want hash you can't have pound – and the reverse in America. The code for ']' in English or American is ä in Swedish and ü in German. The upshot is that you cannot keep a database with words in it from more than one European language. It is all very annoying. No doubt the Americans who invented ASCII found it weird enough that foreigners would want to spell in one foreign language let alone two or all of them.

The person who drew this problem to my attention was an Englishman who wanted to keep a database of military publications. His authors came from all nations under the sun, but he found that if he were to use a computer he could not spell their names properly. No doubt the micro revolution will purge European languages of their idiosyncratic characters.

If you work in Arabic it is possible to assign byte codes to the characters of your alphabet. If Chinese or Japanese is your poison, you can give each character two bytes and so cope with 256^2, or 65 536 of them.

However, what we want most of the time is to store letters and numbers from our own language and this can be done very conveniently in the form of bytes. The computer will keep them in a file on the disk. In small machine operating systems, like MS-DOS and CP/M, a disk file is a very definite thing: a long string of bytes. It has a name and a length. The database manager will keep its information in one or more data files. It will almost certainly keep indexes to the data in separate files and may well keep other little bits of information in other files still.

Not only data gets kept as files. The machine will keep its programs in the same form, and those programs will need subsidiary files. If you use the directory command on your machine you will see a great mass of files with names of the form 'xxxxxxxx.yyy'. The 'xxx' part is the filename, and 'yyy' the extension. The extension tells the user and the computer what sort of file it is. Programs usually have '.COM' or '.CMD' extensions because they can command the computer. Text files often have '.TXT' extensions, databases '.DAT' and so on. The extension is useful because you can make the machine display, copy, print or whatever all files of the same type. For instance the chapters of this book consist of a set of files on my computer called: C1.B, C2.B, C3.B,. C8.B.

The '.B' extension means I can back up the whole book with a single command: 'COPY *.B B:' (copy all the files with the extension .B to disk drive B).

The database manager gets at the files through the 'operating system'. This is a piece of software that lives in the computer and does all its basic housekeeping tasks, like getting files on and off the disk, getting characters from the keyboard, printing on the screen and the printer.

1.3 The operating system

The operating system has an important and quite invisible job to do. It is faced with a tricky problem. When you start out with a new computer and an empty disk, things are fine. You write your first file onto it, starting at the beginning, and from the end of that you write the second. You carry on until the disk is full up and then you stop. There is not a bit of wasted room. But, life being what it is, full of change and bustle, you will have altered the first file. It will now be either longer or shorter than it was originally. If it is shorter there is now an unused space. If it is longer, where do you put the extra chunk? It can't go at the end of the first file because that is where the second file starts.

The answer is to split the disk up (notionally) like a tesselated floor. It is divided into small chunks of between 128 and 1024 bytes each. Each chunk is used to store a piece of the file. (These chunks are, confusingly, called 'records'. We shall spell them with a small 'r' to distinguish them from the human-type units of information – Records – that live in the database. We will meet them in the next chapter.) Whenever a file gets shorter or is erased, some chunks become free somewhere on the disk and can be used for the longer bits of other files. The operating system keeps its own disk directory which tells it what chunks are used in what order by each file. When the program running at the time wants to read a file the operating system automatically gets the records off the disk in the right order and puts them together to present a seamless whole. If a program wants to read only part of a file, it asks the operating system to give it record number so and so from such and such a file. If the program is a database manager and the file the database, it will get the appropriate record number from its indexes (Chapter 2). The operating system will copy the record into a 'buffer' in memory where the program can get at it. A buffer is an area of RAM which can be used as a notice-board, where one program can pin up messages for another. Generally, the bigger these buffers, the better everything works because the number of disk accesses to do any particular job is reduced. But, of course, the space given to buffers has to compete with space allocated to program, so the designer of a database manager has to compromise.

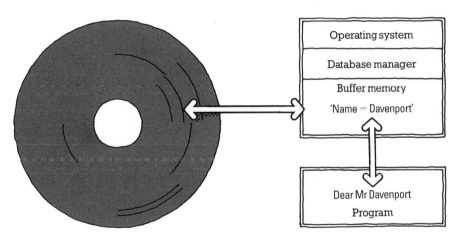

Raw data from the disk is passed through the operating system to the database manager. It can then be accessed by the applications program – here printing a letter.

Programs are said to 'run under' an operating system. Those in common use are: CP/M 80 (for 8 bit machines) , CP/M 86 (for 16 bit machines), MS-DOS, Unix, Idris and Xenix (for 16 bit and bigger machines only) . A program like a database manager will use the operating system to get at its data files. It will be able to ask for a whole file, or maybe just the record that starts at location 100 218 on the disk. The database manager gets the number 100 218 out of its indexes, which are themselves disk files.

A very important quality of the database manager is the speed with which it finds anything. Programmers who write database packages spend a great deal of time and effort trying to maximize this speed. It is as well for the reader, as a possible customer for such systems, to understand what the constraints are on fast searching.

The records are distributed among the tracks and sectors, but only the programmers who wrote the operating system have to worry about that. To find any particular piece of data, the operating system is given the number of a record in a particular file. It looks up in the directory to see where that record is physically on the disk and then moves the head to the right track. It then has to wait for the disk to spin the right sector under it. The head then reads the data off the disk into a buffer in the computer's RAM. The database manager will copy it into its own buffers and maybe ask for the next record if the data Record is larger (as it almost certainly will be) than the operating system record.

The amount of data that can be kept by a database manager depends on the amount of disk space available to be shared between its files. This disk space depends on: (1) the physical size of the disks – and that depends largely on the depth of the purchaser's pocket; and (2) on the largest disk size the operating system will handle. For instance, 8 bit CP/M only allows 8MB.

The maximum practical database will almost certainly be a lot smaller than the available disk space because the database manager has to maintain indexes and it may well use fixed length records which waste a lot of space in empty fields.

1.4 Peripherals

The computer is just a box, a black box if you bought a black computer, otherwise the colour of the manufacturer's choice. (Naive people often think that the shape and colour of the box are important. They say 'Oh, what a pretty computer!' and wonder why programmers spit on the floor. As with Chinese restaurants, good decor is no indicator of good fare.)

If you are lucky the box will have a light or two on the outside to show that it is alive, but in other respects it is not very amusing. What makes it usable is its peripherals: the keyboard and screen (known collectively as the 'console'), the printer and (more rarely) other things like graph plotters. Most desk-top computers are supplied with a screen and keyboard, but if you have a larger multi-user micro you will have to buy separate VDUs (visual display units) .

Even the smallest computers now run database managers. Although Sinclair QL's tape-loop data storage devices are too slow and small for proper database work, it comes with a database package. Here it shows a sample database with worldwide economic data.

COUNTRIES OF THE WORLD

Country: **INDONESIA**   °   Continent: **S.E.ASIA**

Capital: **DJAKARTA**   Currency: **RUPIAH**

Languages: **BAHASIA INDONESIA**

————————————————————— DATA —————————————————————

```
Population ..................... 135.4    millions
Land Area .................... 1919      thousands of square kilometres
Gross Domestic Product ....... 155       U.S. dollars per capita
```

```
>find
"indonesia"
>find
"china█
```

In the days when you bought a 'turnkey' package from a single supplier who would, for a lot of money, install a computer with the programs on it to do what you wanted, you did not have to worry about these things. Now that computers are much cheaper and everyone has to be his or her own untrained and underpaid installation engineer and systems analyst, it has become a problem.

The problem is that most of the time you will be running standard software packages and the authors of those packages could not very well predict which of the thousands of possible screens and printers you might buy. They will therefore provide some sort of set-up program which allows you to configure the software for your machine. It is unfortunate that the most difficult part of getting a computer or a program to work comes right at the beginning when you know least about it. Installing software is a process that sometimes reduces even experienced programmers to a sweaty frenzy.

The minimum hardware configuration for database work includes a floppy disk drive. Here the system has a Quinkey, six key typing pad as well.

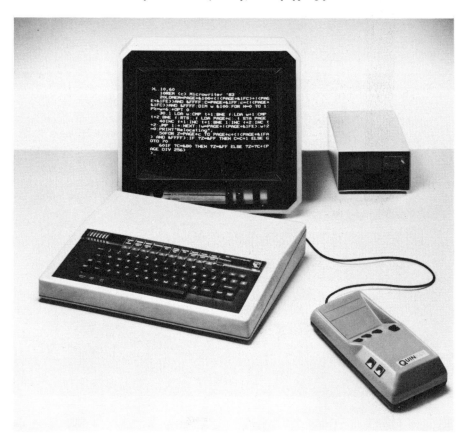

One could write a whole book on the subject, but the things to bear in mind are:

(1) The screen you are using will have its own codes to move the cursor up, down, right, left, etc. If you are lucky the software package you are using will know about the particular screen so you just tell it the VDU's name. If not you will have to enter the various codes, which can be found (perhaps) in your terminal manual.

(2) The printer too will have its own characteristics. Some printers need to be sent a code sequence to tell them to print letter quality or program quality. They may be able to do proportional spacing, in which different letters take up different amounts of room on the paper. 'M' is widest, 'i' is smallest. The alternative is equal spacing like a typewriter. If you are producing tabular work you do *not* want proportional spacing because the result will be wiggly columns.

The IBM PC XT with a built in Winchester disk is suitable for a wide range of database work and runs many database management packages.

Furthermore you will usually have to tell the printer how wide and deep the paper is that you are using (80 or 132 characters wide and 66 lines deep are the most usual). Some printers automatically do a line-feed at the end of each line sent by the computer, some do not. The software has to be able to insert or suppress this. If you are using a printer that can do underlining, bold, subscripts and superscripts, you will have to tell the software the codes to produce those effects. Again, many software packages already 'know' about the popular printers so you may be lucky.

(3) Finally, there is the question of the 'port' – the hole in the computer out of which the data comes and goes to and from the terminal or printer. Most computers nowadays have at least two serial and a parallel port. They will be administered and named by the operating system: you will somehow have to be able to tell the software what port you are using. In MS-DOS the main serial port is called 'COM 1', in CP/M 86 it is 'LST:', in Unix it is '/dev/lp'. If it is a serial port you will have to set up the 'baud rate' – the speed at which data is sent to and from the peripheral. The 'parity' will also be needed – it can be odd, even, mark or space. There can be 1, 1½ or 2 stop bits. The port may use seven or eight bits to the byte. Often the manual does not tell you enough of these things. Sometimes the people who manufactured the system do not know. In five years of computing, I have *never* seen a printer installed in less than two hours. In the worst case there is enough to do to keep one busy for a year.

Future Computers (above left) and Apricots (below left) among others can be networked together to give several people access to the same database. Portable computers (above) give the travelling executive a certain amount of word processing and computing power, plus the opportunity to link into big databases by telephone.

1.5 Mice versus finger tips

Bearing in mind that every computer needs one or two peripherals, that there are millions of computers in the world and that each peripheral costs up to £1500 or more, there is evidently strong commercial pressure on people to invent new peripherals. Furthermore, in the present naive state of the microcomputer market, many customers do not know enough about how the things work to realize that the most important bits – the processor, the RAM and the software – are the least visible.

There has been a continuous flurry on the sidelines of the computer industry to try to get the customers attached to new peripherals. And it is possible that some of them have some merits. One of the oddest is the Micro writer – an electronic version of the American court stenographer's one handed keyboard.

It has a key for each finger and a couple more. You compose letters on it by combinations of key strokes. The inventor claims that it is faster, more accurate, less tiring, more portable etc. It is true that you can detach the keyboard and carry it around with you to enter short documents. It has a processor, some RAM and a little liquid crystal display like a posh typewriter. The *real* selling point is that it looks quite different from a keyboard. Keyboards are what secretaries use and you cannot get red-blooded, rugger playing, male executives to touch them. This is an attitude which people in computing find incomprehensible, but it is very real.

Another device which pretends that you don't need a keyboard, honest, to work a computer, is the 'mouse'. A mouse is an upside down version of the joystick that teenagers use to control Klingons in arcade and computer games. As they wiggle the joystick about, so a cursor or a plane or something moves about on the screen. However, instead of moving a stick, you roll the mouse about on your desk. A ball underneath it turns as the mouse moves and that signals the computer to move the cursor.

The mouse by itself is not much use: it needs to go with software that gives things on the screen to move the cursor to. For instance, in the Apple *Lisa* and *Macintosh* machines, the operating system software paints 'ikons' on the screen to work with the mouse. You have a picture of a wastepaper basket on the screen. Move the cursor to it and press the 'execute' button on the mouse, and the current file is 'thrown away' or deleted. The effect is exactly the same as if you had typed 'DELETE' in a conventional system – and probably no quicker.

Apple's Macintosh is pioneering new conventions of screen presentation.
Instead of typing out program names and commands at the keyboard, the user steers a
cursor round the screen with the mouse until it is over an 'icon' or picture
describing what he wants. He then presses a button on the mouse to get action.

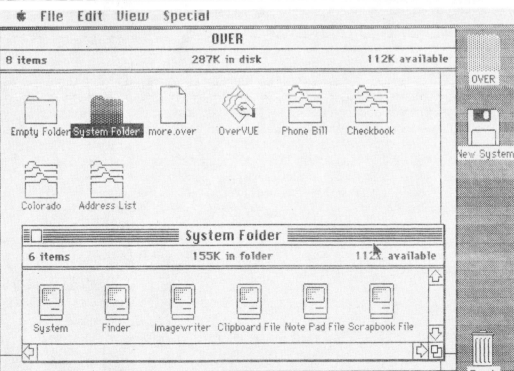

 File   Edit   View   Special

OVER

8 items   287K in disk   112K available

Empty Folder   System Folder   more.over   OverVUE   Phone Bill   Checkbook

Colorado   Address List

OVER

New System

System Folder

6 items   155K in folder   112K available

System   Finder   Imagewriter   Clipboard File   Note Pad File   Scrapbook File

Trash

Given suitable hardware (here, the Hewlett Packard HP 150) the user can indicate a choice to the software by touching the computer screen.

Another way of achieving the same trick is to use a touch sensitive screen. Invisible infra-red beams form a lattice in front of the screen: when you touch the screen at a particular point, two of the beams are broken and a signal is sent to the program running at the moment telling it where your finger is. That can be co-ordinated with the positions of boxes on the screen to convey quite subtle choices. This can be a useful tool for steering people through a database.

An excellent example of software that works well with a touch sensitive screen – or possibly with a mouse – was an airline booking system I saw recently. You began with a conventional table of times, airlines and destinations. You stubbed your finger on the flight you wanted. The touch sensitive screen detected where your finger was and told the software which compared that with the positions of the flights and deduced which one you wanted. The screen cleared and you were presented with a seating plan of the aircraft. You touched it again to indicate whether you wanted first class, coach, smoking, non-smoking etc. The screen cleared again and you were presented with a close-up of the seating area you had chosen with the unbooked seats shown in blue, the booked in red. A touch then selected a seat.

The flight and seat selection process worked very well and much faster than one could have done it with a keyboard. Furthermore the innocent traveller did not have to learn any protocol that a four year old could not master instinctively. 'When you see what you want, touch it' is a scheme we can all follow. But finally you had to resort to the keyboard to type in your name, address and credit card number.

There is a growing passion for computers that can 'speak' and 'hear'. The theory is that you 'just talk normally' to them, they understand and carry out your bidding. There are several serious drawbacks to this scheme. Certainly devices are available which will, if you feed in English text as it might be printed on the screen, produce just-about comprehensible speech. However to make it work properly the programmer has to feed the speaking device rather un-English words. For instance, to make one of them say 'computer' clearly, you had to feed it with 'K UH$_3$ M P U$_1$ T ER'. (The subscripts indicate which of the different sorts of H, U etc. were to be used.) This is pretty heavy on programming time.

Computer speech is also very annoying. A great advantage of letters written on the screen is that you do not have to read them if you know what they say. But if they are spoken each time you have to wait while some grating, monotonous voice says, 'Now please enter your credit card number, taking great care to get it right.' When you have heard the same message fifty three times you are likely to take a hammer to the hardware.

But worse is yet to come. It is much more difficult to turn the grunts and squeaks of spoken English back into text that the computer can understand. Partly this is because people are very sloppy and repetitive – a lot of what they say is 'um', 'er', 'like', 'you know what I mean.' Usually the computer doesn't. This is partly because in order to distinguish between the words 'plaice' and 'place', you have to be able to work out from the rest of the sentence whether the conversation is about fish or locations. And, as yet, computers cannot do this. (Or rather, programmers do not know how to make computers do this.)

I may be cynical and ill informed, but I have not yet come across a talking computer system that worked well or even uninfuriatingly.

We come back to the keyboard which, for all people's efforts to abolish it, will be around for a long time yet. It is, after all, an excellent input medium. It is rich enough to give a wide range of characters (enough to give the whole of Shakespeare, Admiralty Tide Tables and the year's football results), and slim enough to prevent 'in-between' inputs such as occur so often in conversation – the 'um's and 'er's we referred to before.

1.6 Multi-user micros

If it is useful for one person to be able to store and find data quickly and easily, it is much more so for a group of people, who can use the computer not only as an intelligent filing cabinet, but also as a means of sharing information instantly. An excellent example is the office of my own literary agent. He has some 4000 authors who range from the great and the good (literarily speaking) to small fry who write books on computing. He has eight executives who look after different things like book rights in the UK, in Europe, in America. He has specialists in TV rights, plays, films etc. Each author may have two or three projects on hand with repercussions in maybe a dozen different markets. And all these things affect each other. The German television rights for Rosie Blandella's new romance *Fainting Flowers* have just been sold – maybe that will encourage the Brazilian translation rights because Brazil takes a lot of German television shows.

They all work in a charming four floor Georgian house down by the Thames and spend the day running up and down the stairs to look at each others' card indexes to find out what is happening. A database running on a multi-user micro would solve the whole problem because as soon as, say the German television rights were entered on Ms Blandella's Record, the next person to access it would see the information immediately and be able to do the appropriate thing.

Multi-user micros are fairly standard animals. They are either 'multi-tasking' which means that a single computer shares itself among a number of users – like mainframes do – or they are 'multi-processor' which means that a number of independent computers are built into the same box and share the same disk store by being connected to a single, master computer which is usually called the 'file server'. Both these types will normally be accessed through VDUs at some distance from the actual computer. A third technique is to connect ordinary micros together with a 'local area network' or 'LAN'. The upshot of all three systems is that the end-user can look at the same database at the same time as all his or her colleagues.

Unless you have a very powerful micro – and that, at the time of writing, meant one with a 68000 processor – the multi-tasking solution was not really practical. It had been tried on 8 bit machines with the MP/M operating system and was not a success. The ordinary 16 bit processor is not a lot faster than the 8 bit ones and none of them are quick enough to give a number of users the impression that they each have their own private computer. The cost of hardware is so low that the multi-processor solution is

The three basic configurations of multi-user hardware.
In multi-processing (top), each user has his own computer, which gets data from the central disk-server. In multi-tasking (centre) the users share a single, more powerful computer. In a local area network, separate stand-alone computers request data from the disk server.

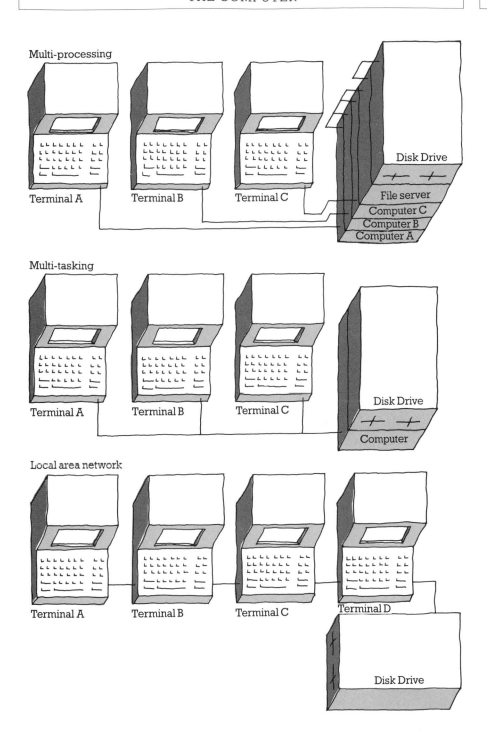

Multi-processing

Terminal A Terminal B Terminal C

Disk Drive
File server
Computer C
Computer B
Computer A

Multi-tasking

Terminal A Terminal B Terminal C

Disk Drive
Computer

Local area network

Terminal A Terminal B Terminal C Terminal D

Disk Drive

much better. Each person has his or her own machine and they share data on the disk – which they can all read at once.

This makes some demands on the software. The crucial problem in a multi-user database manager arises when two users want to alter or erase the same Record at the same time. A multi-user database manager must be able to 'lock' Records to prevent collisions between users.

This means that once the first user has grabbed a Record for alteration, it is marked so that the database manager will not let a second user have access to it. In fact, it returns an error message to the accessing program which means 'Record locked'. It is up to the programmer who wrote the relevant bit of code to decide what to do next – the unlucky user may want to wait and try again or go off and do something else. To control the locking of individual records, the database manager relies on the operating system to lock the database file in some way. A multi-user database must run under a multi-user operating system.

The other, more recondite problem in big computing databases is the 'deadly embrace', which we mention here just for completeness. This happens when two people using a relational database system want to alter a 'virtual' Record* made up of the same two physical Records – R1 and R2. Before the alteration can take place in the virtual Record, the database manager has to lock both physical Records. A deadly embrace arises when user A's software locks R1 and user B's locks R2. Both then try to lock the other Record and of course fail. There are various solutions of which the simplest is to make the software always try to lock the Record nearer the front of the database first. Both users then try to lock the first Record first. The one that fails leaves the second alone (or rather the software does).

1.7 Virtual memory

The traditional distinction between the three main classes of computers – mainframes, minis and micros – is rapidly fading. However, a feature one expects on the more powerful mini that is only just appearing in micros is that of 'virtual memory'. Virtual memory is a hardware facility that lets the programmer ignore the physical size of the machine's RAM. Programs may be written as big as you like and the machine will swap them in and out of memory from disk to give the illusion of RAM many times bigger than it is. Since users demand packages with more and more sophistication, the trend is towards very large programs. In smaller machines, programmers

---

'Virtual' is a useful computing word which means that although the entity it describes seems to be a real thing it is actually made up by the computer out of other bits. In this case the two Records are separate but the user can consider them as a single Record.

have to achieve the same effect by 'paging' chunks of program in and out of memory from the disk as they are needed. This is a laborious and difficult task.

1.8 How computers communicate

A multi-user micro gives a number of users the illusion that each one has a single computer which is – more or less easily – able to share information with the other users' machines. They will all be physically close together and work in and for the same enterprise. Communication is also necessary with other people and enterprises and this too can be done electronically.

The obvious vehicle is the telephone system. In effect a pair of wires runs from your desk to hundreds of millions of other peoples' desks all over the world. There is no reason not to use this network for transferring computer information as well.

Although it can and is done daily, the technology is clumsy. The trouble is that the telephone is designed for voices. When you speak into the microphone you make a voltage that varies up and down in proportion to the loudness of your voice. That voltage runs down the wires and if you are in Britain talking to someone in New Zealand, is transferred by more or less successful methods to the other side of the world. On that and much shorter journeys it will acquire odd noises – whistles, clicks, echoes. The telephone system will reduce the range of frequencies in people's voices so that, although they are recognizable, what you hear is nothing like their real voice in the room with you. It all works adequately enough for voice communication: it is not well adapted for data.

Remember that computers like to talk in 1s and 0s; not at all the up and downs of the voice. The solution is to use a special piece of equipment called a 'modem' (modulator–demodulator) to turn the computer's two binary signals into two musical tones. It whistles down the telephone and the modem at the other end re-interprets the whistles into 0s and 1s. Because the telephone line has so many noises and patches of silence of its own it is not good enough to whistle into the dark and hope that the message gets through. Proper communications modems, or simple ones and the software that drives them, do continuous checks to see that what is sent has actually been received. This is done, in principle, by adding up the 1s in a chunk of message and sending the total – a 'checksum' – as a special part of the message. If the other end has received the message correctly, its total will agree. If not, it won't and it will send a message back saying, 'Don't get you.' And the sending machine repeats. All this happens automatically and invisibly to the user who just wonders why everything is taking so much time. The other bad thing about telephone lines is that they are inherently

A modem turns data pulses into audible tones to send down the telephone line, allowing a remote computer to interrogate a central database.

slow. The maximum speed you can usefully send data down them is 300 baud (roughly bits per second). This means 30 bytes a second or five text words. It takes about half an hour to transmit 10 000 words.

Given better hardware, data can be sent faster and the major telephone services have 'Packet Switched Networks' which transmit data at rates of around 50 000 bits per second nationally and internationally, which is much more like it. You may be able to dial into the PSN through your local exchange, but there is obviously no improvement in speed because you are limited by the local exchange line. If you send masses of data and have a few thousand pounds to spare you can get a high speed connection to the PSN laid to your door. Most of us mortals have to put up with slower methods.

One of the reasons that the advanced telephone authorities are laying optical fibre cable is that it will, in principle, make it possible to bring very fast data links to the customer's door. An optical fibre as thick as a human hair can carry data in the form of light pulses at several million bits per second. This data can be divided up simultaneously into data, television and telephone speech – the last two in digital form, of course.

The modem is often nowadays built into the computer and comes out as a telephone jack. You dial the number you want to send data to, plug in the computer and away you go. Smarter modems can dial the number as well and understand the various tones used by the telephone system to tell you what is happening on the line – number ringing, engaged, unobtainable etc. With the modem will go some software to manage the checksums, do the dialling and possibly to understand the signals the system you are using will send back. See Chapter 6.

1.9 The latest in data storage

If you are interested in database management, you are interested in storing more data than current technology allows. Actually that is rather a simplistic statement. There is no technical limit to the amount of disk storage you can have, providing you feel like paying for it. The database operated by the British Intelligence Service is said to have enough disk storage to keep two or three hundred text words on each of the 55 million inhabitants of the British Isles – some 80 GB (thousand million bytes), and I am sure the Americans far outdo that.

The statement at the beginning of this section should read: 'more than the price of current technology allows you to buy'. Storage is all about price and there is a hierarchy of these prices. The more you pay, the faster you can get at the data but the less you can afford to keep that way. The hierarchy goes:

(1) **Paper in a library**
(2) **Paper in the office**
(3) **Micro-fiche**
(4) **Disk**
(5) **RAM**

Paper will, for the forseeable future, be far and away the cheapest way of long-term archiving. It may well prove to be better than electronics for many shorter term uses too: there seems little chance that we will curl up in bed with a good VDU in preference to a book. A newspaper too is a fine piece of technology and very hard to beat. The great advantages of paper (besides cheapness) are: compactness, portability, the ease with which you can scan a paper database (like the entertainments page in a newspaper) and durability.

Suppose that our whole culture were built around electronic data storage and someone discovered paper. What a technical breakthrough! Storage at fractions of a penny per byte. Input/output technology so simple you don't need any. 'You write to it with a burn stick.' 'You just read it with the eyeball.' 'And the refresh time is a thousand years!' It has to be the greatest product ever.

Enough of fantasy – back to technology. A cross between paper and disk is micro-fiche – miniature photographs of documents. Systems are coming into use in which an index is held by a database manager on disk and hardware automatically finds the wanted fiche. RAM costs, roughly, 3p a text word and gets cheaper and cheaper all the time. But it will not, as far as one can see, be a method for long term data storage for many years. And anyway, every increase in RAM is always gobbled up by the programmers in providing better data manipulation.

The technical developments that interest us database folk lie in disk storage. There are several things happening here and it is difficult – and quite pointless to try – to predict which one will win out at the end of the day.

The general thrust of them all is, of course, to put more data on the same size disk platter. It is important to get the significance of the platter size firmly in mind, because that determines the size of the whole box. The size of the box determines the approximate cost of the thing because high-tech retails at a fairly constant price per pound weight. The size of the box also determines the stroke and reach of the head movement mechanisms. These determine, in part the speed of search of the device. As everywhere else in electronics, cost reductions come not so much from making things of the same size cheaper, but by making things the same size hold more data. And you do that, of course, by making the data storage denser.

To get the basic ideas and problems across, let's consider how one might make an ordinary disk drive hold more. The disposable resource is the area of magnetic medium accessible on the disk surface. We might make the head write nearer to the periphery or to the centre and so enlarge the storage area. The drawback to that is the difference in speed over the rotating disk surface that the head experiences as it moves from the outside to the inside. Each bit of data is written and read in a fixed length of time. At the outside of the disk it occupies a much longer piece of track than at the centre. As the head gets nearer to the middle of the disk, so the ground it covers in a fixed length of time gets smaller. There will be some minimum length of track that gives a satisfactory signal. As the head gets nearer the middle it takes a longer and longer time to write and read data. And that means that the outer tracks are not nearly as dense as they might be.

One solution to this is to make the disk rotate at different speeds when the head is on the outside and the inside. This is what the Sirius (late Victor) does. This scheme gets much more data onto the disk, but it slows access down because the drive has to change speed as the head moves. And this change cannot be accomplished directly: the system has to wait while the disk stabilizes at the new speed before the head starts to read or write data.

Another way to make the drive hold more is to make the head narrower so that it writes a finer track and more tracks can be packed onto the disk surface. Add to that some ingenious data compression techniques and you get 'double density' and 'quad density' disks. This is all very well in principle but since the track is finer the head must be positioned more accurately over it in order to read the data properly. The first symptom of a positioning error is that disks made in one machine cannot be read in another – because their heads are set up some thousandths of an inch differently. Even when different machines have been set up the same, the engineers still have to overcome some horrific problems. The heads have to be in the same position on the disk even when the temperature inside the box changes from freezing to 100°F. This can easily happen if a user leaves a

Disks get smaller and denser. Many new machines have these 3¼" drives

portable computer in the boot of a car over a winter night, drives to work and takes it into a centrally heated office. He or she will be surprised and annoyed if it does not function as stated in the manual.

Another way of increasing data storage is to make the head travel closer to the disk surface. This makes the patches of magnetism smaller and there can therefore be more of them in a given area of disk. The difficulty in doing this with floppy disks is that the disk surface flops about. To get the head nearer you have to have a rigid smooth surface. To prevent dirt getting between the head and the disk, the whole thing has to be hermetically sealed. The upshot is the Winchester or 'hard' disk, and you get more storage with it but at a cost of loss of flexibility. Disks with 5 to 20MB are commonplace. By adding extra disks or 'platters' on the same spindle, 300 MB can be available in a standard 5¼ inch drive.

At the moment all production magnetic disks write patches of magnetism which lie parallel to the disk surface. If the magnetic data were written *through* the disk surface by having the N head on one side and the S head on the other, the same volume of magnetic material could be magnetized in a much lower area of surface. This might give some 30MB of data per 5¼ inch platter or 1200MB of data in a 5¼ inch box.

Another way forward looks like being laser disks. This technology is available now for music recordings and is being energetically adapted for data. In many ways it looks ideal.

The data is written by burning small pits in the disk surface with a

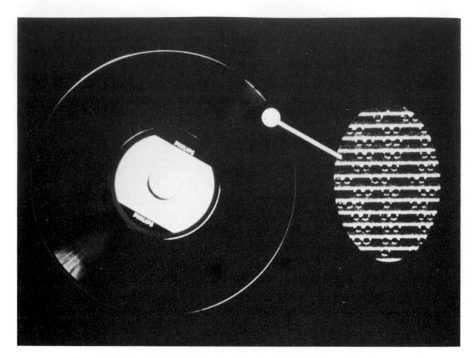

Laser disks under development offer far higher storage capacities.
The laser writes digital data in minute bumps onto the disk surface.

powerful laser. They are read by a low power laser. Nothing touches the
disk so it cannot wear out. Because the pits are so small, the amount of data
that can be stored on a platter is large – a second's worth of high quality
digitally recorded music needs some 50 000 bits, so a little disk that will play
music for an hour will store 22MB worth of data. The bigger disks will hold
some 1000MB.

The drawbacks are also fairly intense. As production technology stands
at the time of writing, laser disks have to be written in the factory. This is fine
for music but no good at all for a medium where users want to create their
own data. Terrific efforts are being put into making writable versions and
some success has been achieved. However, the disks on offer at the
moment are only writable once. You cannot yet re-use the disk surface
again and again as you can with magnetics. But this is not all bad. It pretty
well eliminates the problems of lost files since every version of every file
will always be on the disk. It will only need a small alteration to the
operating system to create a hierarchy of updates, so that one could ask it,
for instance, for the eighth newest version of a particular file.

Another drawback is that the writing process is relatively slow. Instead of
the 20 milliseconds one expects of a medium sized Winchester, a laser disk
may well take some 100–200 ms to write a record. This may be acceptable

for actual data Records – after all, even 200 ms or 0.2 second is a lot quicker than typing a paper document and then filing it. But a database manager, as will be clear by now, does a lot of data writing as part of its own housekeeping, notably in its indexes. If it is going to take this sort of time to write, then the process of entering a new Record and getting all the indexes updated might well take minutes. And experience shows that even five seconds feels like an eternity when your are sitting in front of the keyboard. One solution is to keep the indexes on a Winchester and the data on a laser disk. But a completely indexed database may well have indexes bigger than the data, so one is no further forward. The way round that is to go back to the old idea of 'key fields' and index those. But that spoils the flexibility of a proper database manager.

1.10 Bugs

Every piece of software ever written has 'bugs' in it. A bug is a programmer's blunder: the program does not do what it is meant to do.

The results of a bug are, almost by definition (if such a manifestation of the evil forces of the world can be defined), unpredictable. At the worst a bug in an innocent looking bit of code may wipe all the files on your disk. Or it may be so small in its effects that you do not notice it.

Writing software is like building a card-house. The fact that it is standing now is no guarantee that the whole thing will not fall in ruins in a minute's time. Software goes against all one's experience of life. In the ordinary way if things work at all they work pretty well. If a chair will hold you once it will hold you twice. If a car will run a mile it will run a hundred. If a building stands for five minutes, so engineers and architects tell each other, it will stand for a century. But the fact that one part of a software package works guarantees nothing about any other part. A database manager may have ten thousand lines of code. There may be any number of blunders in each line. Each blunder has to be found and chased out by hand. Sensible software houses employ someone with natural insensitivity and clumsiness to test their software. His job is to do quickly all the stupid things that real live users do given enough time. When the program asks for the price of goods he will type in 'WHY' instead of a number. When it asks the user to type in a letter for a menu selection he will hit Control Z or 53 and watch to see what the program does.

A bug may not be the programmer's fault. The typical program running on a micro today depends on several other programs:

(1) **The operating system.**
(2) **The interface between the operating system and the machine (usually known as the BIOS).**

(3) The language compiler or interpreter used to write the program.
(4) The program itself – which may nowadays incorporate code written by other people and bought in.

All these will have been written by different hands in different places at different times and all will have *their* own bugs.

Not only do all these programs have bugs, they may be latent bugs that only appear when they interact with new versions of other bits of the mix. Thus, a program may work perfectly on the developer's machine. When you put it on yours, using the same operating system it behaves appallingly because it has unearthed some hitherto hidden bug in the software. Transferring software from one machine to another is called 'porting'. It is a very difficult, highly skilled and expensive business. Anyone who tells you that it is easy is lying.

The only defence against bugs is time and experience. Bugs is why new, wonderful, software is inherently undesirable. It will, it *must* have bugs in it, but the passage of time and experience of many users has not found them.

And once bugs are found, practice differs in what software authors do about them. Some houses ignore the whole ugly scene, some content themselves with issuing lists of known bugs and fixing them in new releases once a year or so, others mend bugs as soon as they are told about them. The whole squalid business comes under the heading of 'software maintenance'. Before you buy a database manager and entrust a lot of valuable information to it (how much is a 50 000 Record database at the modest cost of acquiring and entering the data of 20p a Record?) you need to ask very carefully about the user base and the maintenance deal you get.

To be fair, software houses do have a problem. In the old days, software for mainframes or minis might sell 20 or 30 copies at anything up to a million pounds a copy. The user would pay a substantial annual fee for maintenance and the authors could afford to send programmers to the user's site to fix bugs as they appeared. Now, with thousands of people buying software for a few hundred pounds a time – and discounts in the distribution chain may well reduce that to tens of pounds a copy – it is quite clearly impossible to maintain each one individually.

A minor version of the maintenance drama arises in 'support' for end users. Support is what you need when you cannot understand the manual or, having understood the manual, make the thing work. Ideally you want to be able to ring some intelligent person with nothing to do but lead you by the hand through the complexities of a new package. The software house, on the other hand, would just as soon you did nothing of the kind because people capable of giving this kind of help are rare and expensive. The principle seems to be that you should get support from whoever sold the package to you. But this is often a small dealer who cannot possibly understand all the different packages on offer (it takes a professional programmer about a month's hard work to understand one modern software package completely). Before you buy a database manager, establish who is going to tell you how to make it work when you cannot – as will happen sooner or later.

1.11 The cost of software

One significant effect of the maintenance/support can of worms is on the price of software. It is notorious that the price of computer hardware is plummeting. One might imagine that the same thing should happen to software, for after all, software has no real inherent price beyond the cost of the medium that it is supplied on. For instance, a database manager may cost £500. The disk it is supplied on costs perhaps £1. It took someone about five minutes work to copy the software (say £4), and the manual that comes with it costs £5. What happens to the other £490? There are two reasons for this apparent profiteering. Firstly, software is getting more and more complicated. It is very expensive to write and sell. A modern business package will cost about a million pounds to write and two or three more to launch on the market.

Secondly, in the old days, if you bought a computer and a software package from one of the big companies, you would pay an annual maintenance fee. (You still do with serious micro software packages like suites of compilers.) That money would allow the supplying company to pay programmers to answer your silly questions on the telephone and to program out the bugs. It is no longer practicable to collect these maintenance fees from thousands of customers so they must be built into the initial cost of the package.

Furthermore, it is worth paying what might seem an inflated purchase price just to make sure that the software company will still be around later on when you need it.

In assessing what the cost of software ought to be, one ought also to compare the prices charged with the hidden cost to the user of learning how it works. Very few non-programmers can master a business software package in less than three months. That must cost, in wages and lost profits, some £5000. Furthermore, one has to reckon in the cost and value of the data held on the system, which may be much larger again.

1.12 Crashes and backups

In theory data on a disk lasts for ever; in practice it is rather insubstantial stuff. Although magnetism has a self locking property so that individual atoms that try to wander out of line with the others in their patches get pushed back, a small area of magnetism such as is used for writing data will gradually evaporate. This is known as 'byte-rot' in the trade. It is generally reckoned that for perfect results, archived magnetic data needs to be re-recorded every two years.

A much more serious problem is that of 'crashes'. The system is said to crash when it just stops working. This unhappy state of affairs can be caused by a number of things. The simplest is someone switching off the power during a computing operation. The most usual cause is a bug in the software. The nastiest cause is the head wearing away the magnetic material on the disk. But whatever caused the crash, the upshot is likely to be a disk full of scrambled files. Once you have begun to rely on your computer, a crash produces an effect like a kick in the medulla oblongata. The removal of what has become a part of your brain's functioning is uniquely upsetting.

If we were truly philosophical beings, we would expect these annoyances, for computers are spectacularly complicated machines. If the ordinary micro were made of gears and cogs like a mechanical watch, it would easily fill the Albert Hall. It is a miracle that it works at all, let alone that it works perfectly, indefinitely.

In real life all computers crash or 'fall over' from time to time. When this happens it is not unknown for files to get garbled or to disappear from the disk. This is not so surprising when you reflect on the complexity of a file's physical organization, and how easily the operating system can make a mess of it. In any event, prudent computer users assume that their files are going to disappear at any moment. They 'back them up' every day, so that at the worst they will only lose one day's work. If they are lucky, they will be using an operating system like Unix that date-stamps each file whenever it is altered, so at the end of a day one can automatically back up every file which has changed from its last back-up. Once a week they back up *all* their files. They keep last week's back-ups at home and this week's at the office, so that if the office burns down they have only lost a week's work. This sort of backing up is often called 'grandfather', 'father', 'son'.

The hymn writer abjured us 'to live each minute as t'were our last', and the same thing is true of databases, or indeed any computer files. You *must* assume that the computer will devour, wreck and utterly spoil the thing at any moment.

The process of backing up means copying the files on the (usually hard) disk to floppies. Most sensible micros have a utility that manages the tedious business for you. If you are very sensible indeed, you will buy a 'tape streamer' – a device that will copy the whole hard disk straight onto tape in a few minutes.

WHAT IS A DATABASE MANAGER?

A database is simply a collection of lumps of information stored on a computer. The lumps should be similar to each other in shape – though obviously not in content – and there may well be more than one sort of lump (see Chapter 4).

With a database goes a 'database manager', a computer program which organizes the data so it can be found again, accepts it for storage from the keyboard or some other input device and retrieves it when wanted. It does much of the work of a good filing clerk. Generally speaking, you would expect to find the following components in a database manager for a microcomputer:

(1) A core database software package that handles the storage and retrieval of data. This will often be incorporated into an 'enquiry language' (see Chapter 5) which allows the user to question the database.

(2) A screen forms package which allows the user to design and use forms on the computer screen to enter and search for data.

(3) A report generator which allows the user to print 'reports' – that is, lists of records that fulfil some search criterion.

(4) Some sort of interface between the core database package and a word processing package so that the database manager can not only produce lists of names and addresses but also print personalized letters.

Closer links with word processing will be coming soon – see Chapter 3.

However, there is no such thing as a standard database manager. Each package differs from this scheme more or less as its authors think best.

2.1 The intelligent filing cabinet

The database manager is a sort of intelligent filing cabinet which will check information as it goes in and rummage around to get it out. For instance, you might keep a list of names and addresses – a firm's customers, or voters in a constituency. The catalogue of books in a library is another example; so would be the list at Companies House of Limited Companies and their Directors. The first advantage to a computerized database over a paper system is that you can ask it far more varied questions. 'Find me all the books whose author's names start with D, end with E and were published in America in 1952' is the sort of thing which would be quite hard in a paper system but easy with a database. 'Find me all our customers who bought more than £10 000, are in the oil industry and have offices in Berkshire, Herts. Bucks. or Middlesex.'

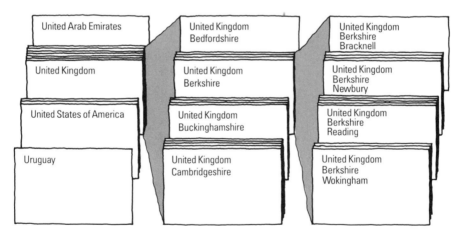

A database is like a card index that retrieves Records by looking for underline in them.

The software package at the core of a good database manager is so complicated that it will almost always be bought from an outside software publisher. When it arrives it will need to be set up* or configured by the end user. He or she will have to tell the system that information about books or, on the other hand, information about customers, will be stored.

*The screen configuration on p. 19 is only part of the story.

It is this configurability that makes database management both more interesting and more difficult than the two major uses of microcomputers that have hit the world so far: word processing (e.g. *Wordstar)* and spread sheet calculations (e.g. *Visicalc).* Programs to carry out either of these functions work much the same no matter what the user is doing with them, and it is therefore much easier to explain to users how to handle them. The way a database manager works depends as much on the way that the user sets it up as on the software itself, so database work necessarily demands a bit more knowledge and commitment from its users.

Another thing that ought to be borne in mind is that the cost of the data can be considerable. It does not terribly matter if you lose a letter or a spread sheet because they represent at most only an hour or two's work. But a database on a modern micro might run to half a million records. If the information in each record cost as little as 10p to get and type in, the complete database will have cost £50 000 – far more than the cost of the hardware and, alas for software publishers, far far more than the cost of the software. It is quite possible that the data is irreplaceable: if you lose it there is no way of getting it back again. If you are going to make an investment like that, it is worth taking some care to look after it.

Enough of warnings. A simple database is usually configured by setting up a 'form' on the computer screen to accept and display information, and a 'report' to print it out. We will go into this in more detail in Chapter 3, and although this appears to the user of the system to be the system, we need to consider now what goes on inside the computer.

The heart of a database manager is a data file which holds your information. A lot depends on how this is organized. For the sake of example, let us look at a database of names and addresses – possibly the most common, though not necessarily the simplest, sort there is.

In the conventional database scheme you first have to decide what sorts of things you are going to store and how many characters long each will be. This will produce the simplest sort of database organization – a 'fixed record system'. Let us keep the following information:

Contents	Size	Running total
First name	10	10
Initial	1	11
Surname	15	26
Address 1	15	41
Address 2	15	56
Address 3	15	71
State	15	86
Zip/post code	7	93

In the file it looks like this:

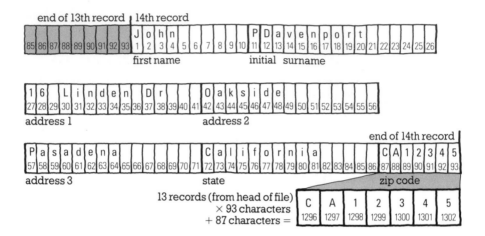

The spaces indicate the unfilled spaces in each item or 'field' as it is usually called (presumably because the field is a fenced off space in which the data item can run about). Notice that the initial 'P' goes right up against the next word, 'Davenport', because the system knows there is only one character there. The zip code field has no spaces because the US Post Office makes zip codes seven characters long (because *its* database is also a fixed record system).

Why does it matter how many characters long the items are? Because it makes it very simple for the computer to find any particular bit of information. Let us say we want the post code of the 14th address in the file. The post code starts at the 87th character in each record and ends at the 93rd. Because the system knows the shape and size of every record, all it has to do is run down $13 \times 93 + 87 = 1296$ characters in the file and there it is. The next seven characters have to be the zip code.

In many database managers of traditional design each field is stored as a separate file on the disk, so that, for instance, all the surnames come together. When you ask it for the 14th Record, the system assembles it by pulling the 14th field out of all the relevant files. This would be called a 'parallel file' system (see Chapter 4).

In real life you very seldom want the 14th Record, you want 'Davenport's' record and you don't know or care where in the database it might be. So, a database manager must have some sort of indexing scheme. In the simplest case, you might decide that you were always going to look up on the surname – just like a card index. The system would then ask you whose record you wanted. You would type in **Davenport** and it would run along

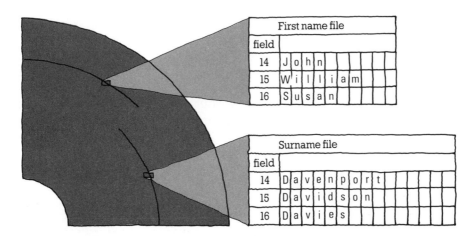

First name file								
field								
14	J	o	h	n				
15	W	i	l	l	i	a	m	
16	S	u	s	a	n			

Surname file									
field									
14	D	a	v	e	n	p	o	r	t
15	D	a	v	i	d	s	o	n	
16	D	a	v	i	e	s			

Traditionally, databases kept different fields in different files on the disk surface. To make up the 15th Record, assemble the 15th fields.

looking at the surname fields (characters 12 to 26) in each record until it found your man.

The surname field would then be called the 'key field' – because it is the key that unlocks the secrets of the database. Only the most antique database managers allow only one key field, because the whole point of using a computer is to be able to search on things *other* than the surname or the invoice number. After all, you can do that with a paper system. Some database packages like dBASE II allow up to seven key fields in a record; others, like Superfile, allow as many as you want. (See Section 3.1 for searching.) This scheme, searching the database one record at a time or 'serially' as it is called in the trade, for the Record you want, is so simple as to be imbecilic. It will also be extremely slow if you have any reasonable number of records.

A better scheme constructs a separate index file for the database. This will have the contents of the key fields, or some short approximation to them, plus the address of the start of each record. Mr Davenport's record started at character 1209. This number is called the 'pointer' to his record, and when you wanted his record you would get the pointer out of the index and then tell your computer's operating system to go to that position on the disk and read in the next 93 characters.

We said that the index might contain some short approximation to the name in the surname field. There is not much point storing 'Davenport' in full when you are going to have to keep it in the main database anyway, so you might as well boil it down shorter to save space and to speed up the time taken to search the index. Your system might reduce the key field in every Record to an intial, three consonants and a pointer: DPRT1209. This is one, very simple and not very practical, method of 'hashing' – and for more on that interesting topic, see Section 2.3.

This fixed record scheme makes life very simple for the programmer who wrote the code for the database manager and rather hard for everyone else. There are three big drawbacks.

When you look at the disk impartially, you see that it is mostly covered in spaces. In fact it will be about half covered since you have had to allow space for the *longest* items you are ever going to store. If you had planned on meeting 'Hanbury-Hancock-Hradislav-Wilson', and then bumped into people called 'Ho' or 'Chow' you might find that almost all your disk was spaces.

This would be annoying because disk storage is still expensive and any number of spaces hardly contributes to your own or the human race's store of knowledge. Moreover, the padding of spaces generally increases the size of the database file, increases the area over which the head must roam and therefore slows down searching. A proper system will be able to store items of different lengths without wasting space. This makes the programming harder, but more than pays for itself on more efficient use of disk space.

In real life, databases keep changing shape. After a few months you find that 15 characters is not enough for surnames and you would like 20; or you realize that the one thing you really wanted to record that would make all the rest worthwhile, was the size of your friends' shoes. But, alas, there is no field to store the information. The only way to make room is to recreate the whole database leaving a gap in each Record for shoe-size to be filled in.

This problem of adding to existing Records becomes much more acute when we think about buying a partly filled database and adding new information to it (see Chapter 6). For example, a company selling sprockle spanners might buy a database of names and addresses of companies which use sprockles and might therefore be interested in buying spanners. This database will acquire more information as the sales reps call – 'Company A wasn't interested; Company B said they will take 50 and to come round on Monday to see the Managing Director.' If they were using a database manager that would not allow its records to be reshaped, they would be in big trouble.

The solution to these and many other problems is the variable record database as implemented in the *Superfile* package. This gives up on fixed fields in favour of markers in the datafile. These are of two types – things called 'tags' which identify the *type* of information being stored – first name, credit rating, telephone numbers etc. – and the physical *end* of the item of information. So, for instance, the name and address we looked at before would be stored at one level as:

...(13th record)
XNAME = John
XNAME = P
SNAME = Davenport
ADDRESS = 16 Linden Dr
ADDRESS = Oakside
ADDRESS = Pasadena
STATE = California
ZIP = CA12345
(15th record) ...

and at the deepest level would look like this:

... (13th record)‹tag1›John‹eoi› ‹tag1›P‹eoi› ‹tag2›Davenport‹eoi› ‹tag3› 16LindenDr‹eoi›
‹tag3›Oakside‹eoi› ‹tag3›Pasadena‹eoi› ‹tag4›California‹eoi› ‹tag5›CA12345‹eoi› ‹eor›
(15th record) . . .

To save space in the database the tags are stored as double bytes, which can take any value between 0 and 65 000. To distinguish them from data characters, they always follow end-of-item ‹eoi› or end-of-record ‹eor› markers and these are bytes with values 253 and 254. To avoid confusion, data bytes are not allowed to go above ASCII 250. (This is not a very onerous restriction, since the ASCII character set stops at byte 127.) The upshot of all this is that no space is wasted on blanks. Items can be any length the user types in and this can often double or treble the effective disk space for ordinary name-and address style Records. Of course, if the user wants to be able to store an optional text field – for remarks, say – which might vary from 0 characters to 5000, there is really no alternative to the variable Record database.

When a Superfile Record is altered, the high level software marks the original version as deleted and copies it – with the alteration – back into the database. The alteration may be a change in the value of an existing Tag, or it might be to add a new tag and value altogether. In this way the system can handle Records that change shape – which is what is often wanted in real life.

2.2 Indexing

All a disk can store is a long string of bytes. The operating system will chop these up into files (see Chapter 1) and the database will consist of one or more files. The principal business of the database manager is then to find the Record the user wants.

It does this by using an index. There is nothing exotic about the idea – it works very like an index in a book or a library. Just as the catalogue to a library is a miniaturized version of the titles and authors of books on the shelves, reorganized to be easy to search; and the index to a book is a miniature version of the book itself (you can get a pretty good idea what a book is about by skimming through the index) rearranged to be easy to search, so the index to a database is a crude version of the main data, reorganized and made smaller.

For instance the index to a book consists of single words along with a page number. The reader then turns to that page and reads through it to find the word of interest. The index to a library consists of (usually) three lists – of authors, titles and subjects – each with a shelf number so that the reader can home in on a small area of the library. He or she then has to search along the shelves and having found a likely book, has to consult *its* index.

Note that the last process in an indexed search is always a serial search. The function of the index is to steer the reader towards a small area of the book or the library. After that serial search takes over.

Note too that the person who arranged the index of the book or the catalogue of the library did work that would otherwise have to be done by the reader. Imagine what you would do if you were faced with a thousand books in the library of an ancient house. Somewhere in some of them are a number of clues to a buried treasure. You do not know what the clues are or how many there might be or in how many books they might be found.

One way of getting the information you want out of the library is to start reading at the nearest book to the door and carry on until you get to the last and hope that you will have noticed the clues on the way. You will be likely to spend the rest of your life wandering about, wondering 'Where *was* that bit about the Armada galleon...?'. A more sensible scheme would be to invest time in reading all the books first, make indexes for them and then a catalogue for the library. Then you will be able to follow up various ideas easily and quickly. This would be called an 'indexed search', where the index leads you directly to what you want.

The point is that the indexer is doing work that the reader would otherwise have to do when looking for some information out of the library. Since a book has only one publisher but many readers it is a sensible

index search   serial search   index search   serial search

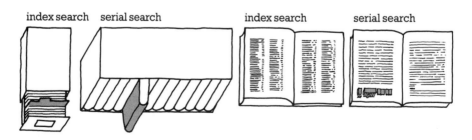

How to find a piece of information in a library using indexed and serial searches.

division of labour to do the indexing before the book even goes to the printer. The same thing applies to a database but since a database has as many 'publishers' as users there is no clear trade-off about indexing. Should you do it when the database is created or when it is accessed?

The programmer of a database manager has a number of options. One option is to index everything in every Record as it goes in and face the certainty that time will be wasted indexing things that no one will ever look up. This means that people entering or altering data will have to wait while the machine indexes what it has just been given.

Another option is to collect all the new data in a pool and index it at night when everyone has gone home. Or to defer the whole problem until the questions are asked and then make the program rush around looking for an answer, so that enquiries take time at the expense of entries. The usual solution is to index most things on entry.

Another problem in a database system is the sheer size of the indexes. The indexes in a book tend to be about 1% of the text, but in a computer system we have the chance of indexing much more finely. For instance, few books index sums of money. A database manager should let you look up every occurrence of £45.67, or find every sum of money between £40 and £50. This is fine and useful, but the penalty is a bulky index. In small computer systems people seem to think that the indexes are somewhat large when they get to be bigger than the database itself.

In practice, database designers compromise like human beings everywhere. They index some things and let others slide, so that some kinds of search will be fast and others slow. The easy way to split the options is to index single words or numbers and to ignore running text. This fits in reasonably well with the ways databases are actually used, it keeps indexes small and makes look up acceptably quick. Often users can guarantee that they will never want to look Records up on certain fields. An index of the remaining fields will, obviously, be smaller and faster to use. It is normally (in so far as there is any normality in this business) called a 'minor index'.

2.3 Hashing

If you want to read about Nixon in a book on American politics, you turn to the index, find the 'N's, look along until you find entries like 'night sittings in Congress', 'Nixon, Richard', and then start to read carefully. The index contains the actual word you are looking for. In computing, things are done differently.

What we need is a number which tells the disk head where to go to get the data Record we want. In a book index you start at the first page and skip along looking for the initial letters you want. Then you fine down. In a computer we want, at all costs, to avoid this kind of serial search where you start at the beginning of a file and womble along it to find what you want. In the paper index you could only work out where to go to find references to 'Nixon' by knowing what came beforehand. You can only know what comes beforehand by looking. Ideally, what we want is a way of working out where to find 'Nixon' without knowing anything else about the contents of the book or database. Librarians do this with the Dewey decimal system. You look at the book, work out its Dewey code number, check that against a map on the wall and that takes you straight to a shelf position. In computing this is done by 'hashing'. Some sort of operation is applied to the word 'Nixon' to produce a number. The index consists of a table of those numbers attached to pointers or disk addresses, so that you can find out where a Record is without having to bother much about any of the rest of the contents.

The process of turning 'Nixon' into a number is called 'hashing' presumably because it has as little respect for the original shape of the word as a hamburger chef has for the shape of a cow. There are as many methods of hashing as there are programmers. One of them might be to take the ASCII value of the first letter divided by 10, add to it the ASCII value of the second divided by 100, the value of the third divided by 1000, etc. This produces results like:

Word	Hash value
NIXON	8.62668028447502
ANTIDISESTABLISHMENT	7.372062127717147
ANTIDISESTABLISHMENTARIANISM	7.372062127717147
YRUFGCUSUS	9.812786103029187

In some ways this is quite a good scheme because it guarantees that each word will have a different hash value – providing the software that does the sums can handle enough digits. But it is not so good because it saves vast amounts of space for letter combinations that are not words at all, like the fourth entry. The ideal hashing system gives each word that the users want a unique value – and wastes no space on words or letter combinations they do not want. In real life this ideal is unattainable, and real hashing schemes will always waste space on words that no one will ever use while having to accommodate collisions where two or more words they do want produce the same hash value – like the second and third here. In theory they should not occur, but in practice collisions are produced – as here – by a lack of precision in the MBASIC interpreter that calculated the hash values. Or, the algorithm that produces the hash values may not discriminate between all words that occur.

The design of algorithms to do hashing is a very difficult and specialized job which we cannot begin to examine here. To do it properly needs a good grasp of statistics and the way languages work. Knuth (1973) points out that only one in 10 million of the mathematical functions that turn a word into a number will actually be suitable for use in hashing. He goes on to illustrate the difficulty of producing unique values using the example of the 'birthday paradox'. You can hash a person by taking his or her birthday. With 365 days of the year to choose from, people ought to be well separated. But the famous paradox says that if you have no more than 22 people in a room the chances are good that two of them will have a birthday on the same day of the year.

Having got a hash value we can then use it to find a position on the disk. We might say: our disk holds 10 million bytes. We will allow 20 bytes for a single word entry – that gives 500 000 positions and we can find any one of them directly, knowing its number. The number is then a 'pointer' to the position. The smallest hash value is that of 'A'; 6.5. The largest is that of 'ZZZZZZZZZZZZZZZZZZ'; 10.00000010689103. We can just divide the disk up in those proportions and immediately calculate a disk position for each word. This is easy and quick but again it leaves vast amounts of space that will never be used – like the slots for 'ZZZZZZZZZZZZZZZZZZ' and 'YRUFGCUSUS'. Even the slot for 'ANTIDISESTABLISHMENT' is unlikely to be filled in most people's systems but if it were, 'ANTI-DISESTABLISHMENTARIANISM' would land right on top of it. This sort of problem inevitably arises in any practical hashing scheme. It can be dealt with by providing a pointer in the landed-on value to extra, overflow values which can each, in turn, point to more.

This indexing scheme is rather like a shelf map that works for all libraries everywhere. Dentistry is, in the Dewey cataloguing system, decimal number 617.6. In a totalitarian state you could, presumably, pass a law that the first book on dentistry is to be shelved 1000 feet from the first book in the library. That would mean that a small country library would have to build miles of shelving it had no books to fill, while a national Library like the Library of Congress or the British Museum would have no room for all its books on things like debt collecting.

While it would be wonderful to have an indexing scheme that could ignore what was in the rest of the database, in real life we have to fit each word or entry into the context of all the others. As in a library, we have to have a shelf map which takes into account everything else in the library. And that imposes a lot of work on the indexing part of the system because essentially it has to sort the database. It has to find where each new entry fits into everything that is already there. This, as we shall see, is laborious.

2.4 Serial indexes

The simple way to handle indexes is to produce a miniature version of the database and to search it from one end to the other when we want to find anything.

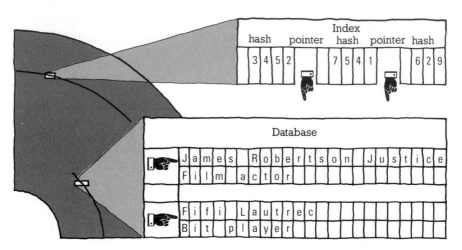

Here we have a database of film players, consisting of first names, surnames and a brief description. For simplicity we assume that only the surname is indexed. The result is that a hashed version of the surname appears in the serial index, along with a pointer – p1, p2 – to the position of the start of the Record in the database file. To find Fifi Lautrec, the database manager hashes her surname, using some more or less clever algorithm, to the value '7541' (we are not concerned at the moment with why it turns 'Lautrec' into '7541'). It then runs along the index file looking for '7541'. When the database manager finds this hash value it looks at the pointer, p2, and jumps to that address in the database file. It will check the entry in the database to make sure that it is actually 'Lautrec', as requested. It has to do this because any practical hashing system that does not produce vast gaps will also produce the same hash value for several different words. 'Lautrec' produces '7541' but 'Constanza' might also, so the database manager has to make sure. If the name matches then the database manager produces the Record for the user's delectation.

The important thing about any database operation is how long it takes. Here the big 'overhead' is searching the index. It sounds simple enough, but what actually happens is quite complicated.

In order to search the index for '7541' the index file on the disk has to be copied into the computer's memory. That involves positioning the disk head at the start of the index file and reading a section of it – not all, because it is almost certainly too big to fit completely into RAM. The memory space it is copied into is called a 'buffer' – computerese for an area of memory reserved for chunks of text or data. Once it is in RAM, a piece of code runs along it looking for the first character of the hash value – '7'. If the first character of the hash value in the index it is looking at is not '7' there is obviously no point comparing the other three characters so it moves on. When it finds an initial '7', it tries the next character '5'. If that matches it tries the next, if not it moves on. At the end of the buffer it reads in another chunk of index and tries again.

Generally speaking operations in memory are quick. What takes time is moving the head around the disk and reading in chunks of file. So, the bigger the buffer available the fewer individual disk operations and the quicker the indexing will work.

The other time-consuming operation is verification – checking Records with the right hash values in the index to make sure that they do have the right name. Again, this takes a disk operation – moving the disk head to the pointer position and reading in the Record – and takes time. The coarser the hashing, the more often this will have to be done. By way of example, let us suppose that we have 100 000 actors in our database and that all of them have different names. Our hashing algorithm produces four decimal digits, so there can be only 9999 different hash values. But there are ten times as many names as this in the database, so it follows that on average, each hash value has to serve ten different names.

On the face of it this means that the search for any particular name in a single file will incur about ten verifications, but things are not quite so bad. Once the real name has been found, the searching stops. The real name is as likely to be at the beginning of the database as at the end, and will be, on average, around the middle. This cuts the verifications down to five. It follows that the finer the hashing the fewer the verifications, and you get finer hashing by including more characters in the hash value. Another decimal digit would reduce the average number of hits per hash value from ten to one, apparently speeding up access by a factor of five. However, it would increase the size of the index file by 25%, include more pointers and impose a quarter more disk accesses to read the index into its buffer, so that would slow things down again. It would also make the index bigger in relation to the database, but since disk space now is cheap in comparison with peoples' time, this does not matter so much.

2.5 B-tree indexes

The noxious being lurking in the serial woodpile is the necessity for searching through the whole index in order to find any particular Record.

We can do better than that. When you look for someone in the London telephone book you do not start with the first entry '001 Anglia Trade Protection Ltd' and read on through the whole epic. If you want to look up the Norwegian Technical Translation Company's phone number you go about things in a much more sensible way. You ignore the cream coloured book (A to D), the pink book (E to K) and grab the green one (L to R). You flip through it until the heavy type at the top of the page starts showing 'N's and then 'No's. At that point you put on your glasses and start running your finger down the fine print.

Our experience of telephone books and the reasonably sensible way they are put together* makes it easy to get a pretty good idea of where to embark on the inevitable serial search which must start at some point. The secret of fast searching is to postpone the onset of serial examination of the data.

In searching the index for the hash value '7541', we could have speeded the thing up by dividing the index in much the same way as the telephone book. One simple scheme would be to divide the single index file up into ten smaller files, one for each of the initial digits. We would then store '5418' in the seventh file – meaning that the hash value began with '7'. This apparently makes the file smaller because we are no longer storing the first digit in each hash value. However, it has to be replaced by a pointer and a filename so the effect is illusory. However there is a real economy of time to be had in searching this subdivided index, because to look for '7541' we go to the seventh file and search for '541'. The time that would have been taken to search the other nine files is saved, which reduces disk access, and the number of characters that have to be compared to find a match is reduced by 25%, which speeds up processing.

There is no reason to stop there: we can apply the same principle to the second digit as well – and to the third and to the fourth.

This works better but is wasteful of space because although there are only ten pointers at the first level – corresponding to the four figure hash values starting 0,1,2,3,...9 – each of those points to 100 at the second level, 1000 at the third and 10 000 at the fourth – which is the same size as the original serial index. This combined index is bigger by 1110 or 11% than the original, plus the extra pointers. However it will be much faster to access because the computer has to make, at most, four disk accesses before it comes up with a pointer to a database Record.

In the early days of database management people were very dependent on the actual hardware configuration of their computer. The various levels of these indexes corresponded to the track, sector and record numbers of

*Setting aside the Paris telephone book which indexes a large number of people under 'M.' and 'Mme.'.

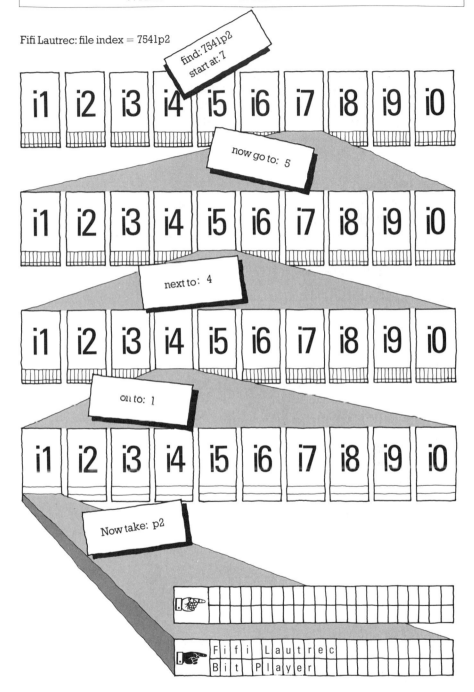

The principle of the 'Indexed Sequential Access Method' (ISAM): an index at each level leads to 10 subsidiary indexes, whether they are full or not.

the actual data on the disk. It was then called 'Indexed Sequential Access Method' or 'ISAM' for short. Today, when people talk vaguely about ISAMs they seem to mean some sort of multi-level, fixed length indexing method.

We can look at levels 1,2 and 3 as indexes to the fourth level whose use greatly speeds up retrieval of specific Records. Because a few entries at the root spread out to a large number at the bottom, this sort of organization of data is called a 'tree' – even though it is presented upside down. A notional branch splits off at each entry and is called a 'node'. The topmost nodes, the direct pointers into the database, are called, continuing the arboreal simile, the 'leaf nodes'.

This is not the most efficient method of indexing since it is rather inflexible. Each of the 10 000 possible hash values has its set of holes. If they are not filled by the way the actual algorithm works, space will be wasted. Again, in real life, a hashing algorithm will be capable of producing many million of entries, only some of which will be used, so it would not be possible to provide each of them with a space in this way.

Instead, advanced database managers now use a system called a 'B-tree' index. ('B' stands for balanced – the tree is symmetrical so that all paths

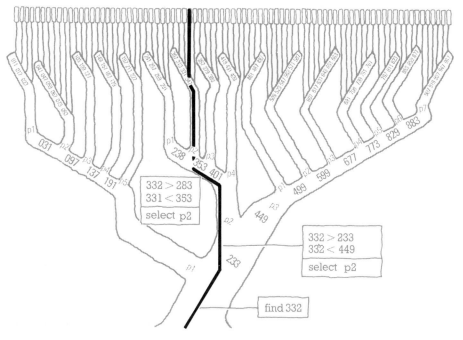

In a 'B-Tree' (balanced tree) index, only filled spaces are stored, improving speed and compactness over ISAM.

through it are the same length.) This has the same fundamental structure except that it is more flexible. At each level, or in each node, a B-tree holds a certain number of hash values and pointers. The hash values are sorted into order so that they get bigger from left to right at each level.

To find the leaf with a particular value – say 331 – you start at the root. The root contains: p1, 233, p2, 449, p3. The value 331 is bigger than 233 so you skip over p1, and less than 449 so you select p2, (The pointers – p1, p2 etc. – are of course different at each level.)

The pointer p2 points to a node that contains: p1, 283, p2, 353, p3, 401, p4. The value 331 is between 283 and 353 so you select p2 again. And so on until you get to the bottom and the pointer into the database file. The main point about a B-tree is that the nodes are very seldom full. If you want to insert a new piece of data with its pointer into the database file, you put it in the lowest node in the right place. If that fills the node up you split it into two half full nodes and insert an extra pointer in the level above. If that fills that node up you split and move up one as before. There are considerable refinements on the basic idea. See Knuth (1973).

All this is important, but mainly of interest to the systems programmer who tends to regard data as a string of bytes with no particular internal meaning. The game that is played is to store and find a string as quickly as possible. The end user sees it rather differently. That string is a number – the price of Pork Belly Futures. Or it is a piece of text – an account of the sinking of a Spanish treasure galleon, or an estimate of the reliability of an employee. Indexing software makes a distinction between numbers and text. It has to be able to index numbers in a sensible way so that, for instance, the hash values of 1 and 2 are not too different, while 999 999 999 is miles away.

Words present different problems – one might want text starting with 'A', or containing 'drinker' (if you are thinking about people not to send to Saudi Arabia). The obvious thing is to assume that each field has one word in it and index that. But in practice many fields have more than one word. One scheme is to index the first substantial word – if there is one – so that 'A. K. Jones', 'Mr Jones', 'Dr Jones', 'Sir Jones' are indexed as 'Jones'. In practice a sensible database designer would remove the initials and titles into separate fields so that the indexer would just have to cope with a surname field 'Jones'. Things get tougher when you try to index running text such as: medical notes on patients, news stories, digests of books and papers in a library system.

There are two problems involved in indexing running text – what does the reader actually want to know, and how to find the room to store it. These interact on each other. It is not satisfactory to treat the text in the same way as a word field. If you did, this paragraph would be indexed on its first substantial word: 'problems'. Which happens not to be too bad, but it wouldn't be very helpful to go to the index of this book and find the bald entry 'Problems p55'. Problems with what?

It would not be any more help to index every word in the paragraph either. Imagine a database that would return every occurrence of 'the' or 'a'. Well, you could tell it not to, and it is true that the interesting words occur less often than these but there is no cut-off point. You cannot say that the little boring words occur more often that $x\%$ and we should therefore index the rarer ones. Even if you could, this procedure would, for instance, produce an index entry on 'therefore', which would not be a lot of use either. The obvious thing is to try to help the human indexer of text. He – or more usually, she – reads through the stuff and marks the words which another reader would find useful. The automation of help can be done in two stages. In the first stage the human indexer has to read the text, but has some way of marking words for indexing. The system will then hash them and put the values into the B-tree with a pointer to the Record that holds the surrounding text.

A variation on this is for the human indexer to start off by producing a list of words that will officially be 'key' words. The database manager then searches the text in question for any occurrence of the key words. For instance a database maintained by an oil company of its many exploratory wells might include a chunk of text in each record which describes the geological structure at the site. Before the first well was drilled, let alone described in the database, the person who set up the system decided that words like 'lignite', 'oolite', 'dipping fault' would be worth indexing. This use of a predefined list of indexed words makes sure that users know that the words they are looking for have been indexed, if they are in the database at all.

The second stage is to try to produce some automatic way of selecting words to index. The only promising method so far seems to be to calculate the frequency of every word in the text and then to compare those frequencies with the frequency with which that word appears in 'ordinary' text. 'Key' words tend to be repeated more often in the text to which they are keys than 'ordinary' words, and so can be identified. It may be necessary to get the human indexer to edit the index afterwards.

Finally, having in some way indexed our text by key words, we need some way of working backwards from the complete list of key words we would like satisfied. We might be searching in a news database for 'riots', 'US Embassy', 'child', 'broken leg', 'Marine', for a story in which a small girl was rescued from a riot by a gallant Marine and carried into the Embassy to have her broken leg treated. We might search with the whole list and fail to get a match because in the actual story we want, the broken leg was described as an 'injury'. The database manager ought, therefore, be able to drop key words and re-search until it gets at least one match. Ideally, the system would have a 'thesaurus' that would recognize synonyms and search on them. However, this is looking a good way into the future.

2.6 To sort or not to sort

Life would be much easier for people who write database managers if people who use them did not want to see their data sorted. 'Sorted' means printed out with various fields arranged in numerical or alphabetic order. For example:

Albert	Albertson	12 Alpha St.	Athabaska
John	Albertson	12 Alpha St.	Athabaska
Susan	Briant	2 Alpha St.	Athabaska
Arthur	Aske	223 Benson Ave.	Athabaska
...			
Herbert	Zelig	1 Unnamed Dr.	Washoe

where the right hand fields have precedence over the left hand ones, i.e. they are 'nested'.

It is important to distinguish between *sorting* and *selection*: a telephone book is *sorted* by surname and if it were not it would be so much waste paper. However, if you had the contents of the telephone book in a database you could *select* not only on surname but also on street or telephone number. There is no need for the database to be sorted since its indexing mechanisms will produce whatever you want dynamically.

So sorting and printing go together, and one can hope that as paper loses its importance as a vehicle for communication, so sorting will fade away too.

Why am I so against sorting? Mainly because it takes a long time. You only have to sort a pack of cards into ascending suits to see why this is so. As you deal each card off the top of the unsorted deck you have to search the sorted deck to find the right place to insert it. You have to do a lot of looking to get it right. And the computer has to do the same thing. The process of inserting each unsorted item into its right place in the finished list requires a great deal of searching. 'I'm holding the three of hearts – now, where are the hearts? Where is the two or four? Can't find them. OK, look for the Ace or the 5...'

A pack of cards is simple because you know how many there are. You could draw out, on a big piece of paper, where each card should go, deal the pack into its proper places and then pick it up again. But most databases are not as simple. You might be sorting names and addresses by surname, street and town. You do not know in advance what should go where: the position of every address depends on every other address. A simple-minded sorting program has to compare every address in the list with every other. If there are n addresses, it has to do n^2 comparisons. If you are sorting a hundred or so addresses which can all live in the computer's RAM, then this will be quite fast. But if you are sorting several thousand or even hundreds of thousands of addresses, then they must be kept on disk. Each operation involves getting two addresses off the disk, comparing them and putting them back in the right order. Suppose we have 1000 addresses and each disk access – to bring an address into RAM for comparison – takes 0.033 second (reasonable for a small Winchester). The whole process will take $1000 \times 1000 \times 0.066$ seconds (ignoring the time taken in RAM for the actual sorting) and this is 16.66 hours. Ten thousand addresses will take a shade under ten weeks.

Bearing in mind how fond people are of sorted data, it is just as well that cleverer strategies are available. The best theoretical performance for a program sorting n items with each sort operation taking one second is $n \times \log(n)$ seconds. This may not seem very encouraging unless you are a mathematician, but it reduces the time to sort 10 000 addresses to an hour and a half. Writing such a sort program is not at all easy, and there are whole libraries on how to do it.

A database can be sorted many ways at the same time. You might want a list of customers sorted by name, town and county, and also want them sorted by age and size of debt. Obviously the physical file cannot be sorted two ways at once (as a pack of cards cannot simultaneously be sorted with all the aces together, all the two's together *and* into suits.) Instead, separate files of sorted pointers or indexes are created. The software can use them to produce the database in whichever sorted order is wanted at the time.

Some database managers keep their files permanently sorted. This has the advantage that you can, if you wish, see your customers in, say, invoice number order, but has the disadvantage that whenever a Record is added or altered it has to be sorted into its correct place in the file – which can take a bit of time. Meanwhile the operator has to sit twiddling his or her thumbs. And, of course, it can only be held in one pre-sorted order.

USING A DATABASE MANAGER

The user of a database manager is confronted with the machine and the packaged software. Time and patience will make sense of both.

We have been charmingly vague about what the user actually sees when using a database manager. The words about file structure in the previous chapter are very important, but they are not what is uppermost in the clerk's mind first thing on Monday morning when there is a heap of orders to be entered into the system.

Using a database manager involves two levels of software operations. At the lowest, fundamental level, there is the business of storing and searching for data. At the highest level it needs to be typed in, checked, have calculations done on it and be printed out. We looked very briefly at the storage and retrieval part of the job in the previous chapter. Here we turn our attention to the highest level or 'front end' – what the user sees when running the software.

3.1 Forms (and filling them in)

Logically, the first thing you have to do when you use a database manager is to enter Records. The simplest way of getting them into the machine is to allow the user to type into a *form* on the computer screen. The form is designed by the user and put on the screen by a part of the database manager called a 'forms generator'. This form can be quite like the paper version it replaces. The thing to remember is that the data goes through it like a sieve. The form is only stored once. As the records go in and as they come out again they are presented within the frame of the form. This process creates a 'flat file' – a file of Records which all have the same structure – as distinct from an hierarchical or relational database (see Chapter 4).

A form usually consists of two things: fields and text. The fields are where you type information; the text areas contain notes, instructions, reminders and whatever. Smart programmers often arrange that the two areas shall be in two different styles of screen letter – one will be highlighted and the other not, or one in reverse video and the other normal – and if your screen does colour, one could be green and the other orange. There are many possibilities – but none of them is terribly important.

At first it might seem that the notes telling you what to enter in a field are the same as the tags in Chapter 2. Often this is so: you are asked to type in a company's name in a field described by the word 'Company', when the underlying tag is indeed COMPANY. However, this is not always so. If you were working for the US Immigration Authority, your form might ask you to enter an immigrant's mother's maiden name. However, as far as the database is concerned, this is a SURNAME just like any other.

If your database has fixed length records the screen form will very often show you how long the fields can be by printing a dot or some such for each potential letter, and this dot disappears as you type in your data. Another scheme is to indicate the fields with pairs of brackets the right distance apart: '[ ]'.

Now, as you type in data, is a very good moment to check and control what goes in. The trouble with computers is that the information in them is invisible and acts fast. If you make mistakes putting it in, you may never see them until the customer complains about receiving a bill for £9 999 999.99. So, a good forms package should not only accept your data for forwarding to the database package at the core of the database manager, it should carry out a lot of checks on it as well.

There is no standard list of these checks, but the sorts of things people want to do are:

(1) *Dictionary look-up.* You are an insurance agent. You sell a policy written by Standard Life of Canada. You don't want to have to type in the whole rigmarole of their name and address each time – because it happens ten times every day. You just want to enter 'SLC' and get the database manager to look up the name and address for you and enter it in the Record you are creating. Although this sounds simple, it raises issues relevant to the relational databases discussed in Chapter 4.

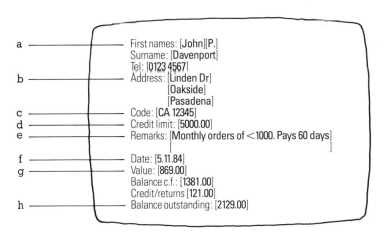

```
                              Tag    Value
                    ┌─ FNAME = John ──── Data items not padded
                  ┌─┤  └─ FNAME = P
  Repeated Tags  │    SNAME = Davenport
                  │  ┌─ADDRESS = 16 Linden Dr
                  └─┤  ADDRESS = Oakside
                     └─ADDRESS = Pasadena
                         ZIP = CA 12345
                         TEL = 0123 4567
                      CREDIT = 500
                    REMARKS = Monthly orders of <1000. Pays 60 days
                        DATE = 5 11 84
                       VALUE = 869.00
                       BALCF = 1381.00
                         RET = 121.00
                     BALOUT = 2129.00
```

Some characteristics of the underlying Superfile Record (above) and its screen presentation (below). The Record gives a simple format for information storage and interchange between people, machines and programs. It consists of 'tags' (left) and 'values' (right). Together they make up 'items'. New items can be added to a Record at any time, and a database can hold many different Record types. Normally a Record is displayed in a form on the screen.

```
a ─────────────── First names: [John][P.]
                  Surname: [Davenport]
                  Tel: [0123 4567]
b ─────────────── Address: [Linden Dr]
                           [Oakside]
                           [Pasadena]
c ─────────────── Code: [CA 12345]
d ─────────────── Credit limit: [5000.00]
e ─────────────── Remarks: [Monthly orders of <1000. Pays 60 days]
                           [                                     ]
f ─────────────── Date: [5.11.84]
g ─────────────── Value: [869.00]
                  Balance c.f.: [1381.00]
                  Credit/returns [121.00]
h ─────────────── Balance outstanding: [2129.00]
```

(a) Repeated first name fields
(b) Repeated address fields
(c) Numeric telephone number field
(d) Credit limit controlled between 10 000 and 100
(e) Text field for remarks
(f) Automatic date conversion to number of days since 1st Jan, 0 AD
(g) Money fields, controlled between 1000 and 0
(h) Calculation field to add up balance and value and subtract credit/returns

(2) *Verification.* All data can be verified by forcing the operator to type it in twice. The first entry disappears and the operator has to retype it in exactly the same way. If there is any difference the entry is rejected. This catches careless typing mistakes – at the cost of some irritation. You would probably only use it for things like insurance policy numbers.

(3) *Range checking.* The package should be able to check that a number is, say, money (with two decimal places) and lies within a range, set when the form was designed. For instance, a domestic electricity bill might reasonably be expected to be between £0 and £1000. If the operator carelessly typed in 34 567 instead of 345.67, this check would catch the error.

(4) *List checking.* The corresponding process for text data is to check against a list. For instance the database might be concerned with the maintenance of a truck pool. Whenever a truck gets greased, an entry, including its licence plate to identify it, is made in the database. It would be a good idea to make sure that this licence plate is in fact one of ours and that we are not maintaining some spurious interloping truck. The package should therefore be able to take the entry in a specified field and check it against the database to make sure that the same information is there somewhere already. A pleasant refinement to this is to make it so you only have to enter the first few letters of a piece of stored text and it comes up in full – this is much the same as dictionary look-up.

The inverse test is also handy: to *reject* what is already in the database. This would be useful when entering insurance policy numbers which are all supposed to be different.

There are often fields whose contents will be displayed but must not be altered. A read-only feature, which will not allow the user to enter or alter data is therefore handy. A whole form may be read-only.

Dates need to be checked for validity and often also need to be converted into a 'day number'. It is quite difficult, for instance, to work out the days, 30 days from the date of an invoice, when the payment comes due. More complicated calculations on dates often have to be done and the simplest scheme is to turn each date into the number of days since some arbitrary, long-ago day. A date that is often chosen is 1st January, 0 AD. For no terribly good reason that I can see, a day number like this is usually called a 'Julian date' after Julius Caesar. Well, he did invent the modern calendar.

Since the software has to know that February has 29 days in leap years unless the year is divisible by 100 in order to calculate the Julian date, it might as well check that the date typed in makes sense in all other respects.

3.2 Computer security

Security has two meanings in computing. The most important one is about the physical safety of your data, and we have covered that in Chapter 1. The less important one – at least in microcomputing – is keeping unauthorized people out of your system. Perhaps this is because the machines are so unreliable that intruders are unlikely to find anything useful there when they break in. In my experience of selling database software to some very hush-hush as well as many ordinary people, security in this sense has never been a real issue. However it probably will be and we had better deal with it, particularly since the UK Data Protection Act may make it a criminal offence to leave computerized personal data lying about where anyone can look at it.

The standard sort of security scheme is to control access to the system or particular pieces of data by passwords. When you boot the system or enter the database manager, you are asked for your password. You type it in, and for once the screen does not print the letters. Experience shows that it is very difficult to see what word someone has typed just by looking over his or her shoulder at the keyboard – and of course if nothing appears on the screen there is nothing for the over-the-shoulder peeper to learn. Password schemes can get quite complicated. One reasonably effective system is to have several levels of protection – say 1,2,3,4 and make them apply either to whole Records or to fields. What is a protection level for data is a clearance level for people, so someone with level 4 clearance can look at all data. Someone with level 3 clearance can look at data with 1,2, or 3 level protection. There will normally be two different protection systems: one to control the reading of data; the other to control writing. A person may be allowed to read certain things but not to write to them or change them. On the other hand, that person may be allowed to write data but not to read other items in the same file. In big relational systems running on mainframe systems, the permutations of security accesses can become bewilderingly complicated (see Date, 1981).

Your clearance level is established by your password. Of course, a database with protection has to be encrypted otherwise anyone can get at the data just by using the operating system to print out the database file.

The key person in a security system is the 'System Manager', the person who holds the master or system password and who controls all the rest. If the System Manager is careless and leaves the master password written on the wall over the terminal everyone is in big trouble.

In mainframe computers, particularly those that are connected to the public telephone network, security is a real problem. The papers often carry stories about droll teenagers who break into banking computers and credit themselves with a trillion dollars or who precipitate World War III and other jests. Happily in the world of microcomputers this is less of a problem because physical access is usually controlled by access to the building where they are installed or to the group that uses them.

3.3 Speedy answers

The whole point of keeping a database on a computer rather than on paper is to be able to search it quickly and on many different criteria. If the database manager cannot do this, then frankly, it is *no good*. How do you tell if it is searching fast enough? This is yet another version of the 'How long is a piece of string?' question which most computing problems turn into. It depends who is waiting for the answer and why.

Imagine that we have a database system which is used by a telephone operator. People ring up to order goods or to see if their loved ones' aeroplanes are late, or to find out if the man they have stopped in the street is a wanted criminal (in this case the people are the police). The operator sits in front of the terminal waiting to read the answer. Systems like this are said to be interactive (meaning that when you question them, you get an answer right back) and are usually expected to do their stuff within a second and a half. Experience shows that the human frame gets discouraged if it has to wait much longer than that and a wait as long as ten seconds is hopeless.

So that sets a limit to the performance of interactive systems. Of course, many database uses do not need quick draw answers like that. If you are printing out address labels for a mail shot or account statements (called 'batch' jobs in the trade) you can let the machine run overnight and tolerate a longer response time. Very often, too, the printer takes longer to print a Record than the database manager to find it, so the database's speed of search is not a problem.

However a database manager can never be too quick. So far we have been thinking about searches for single records: 'What's the ETA of flight 356 from Amman?' which can be answered by putting one search criterion in. In this case you would type in the flight number, and get back a record with the latest information on the aircraft's progress. But, alas, most database work is not as simple as this. Even in an apparently slow batch system we may have to do multiple searches. A database manager with poor performance would slow things up dreadfully.

A major expansion of the usefulness of databases will come when they can store and analyse pictures as well as text and numbers. This page shows how, in a few years' time, graphics databases may help in the fight against crime.

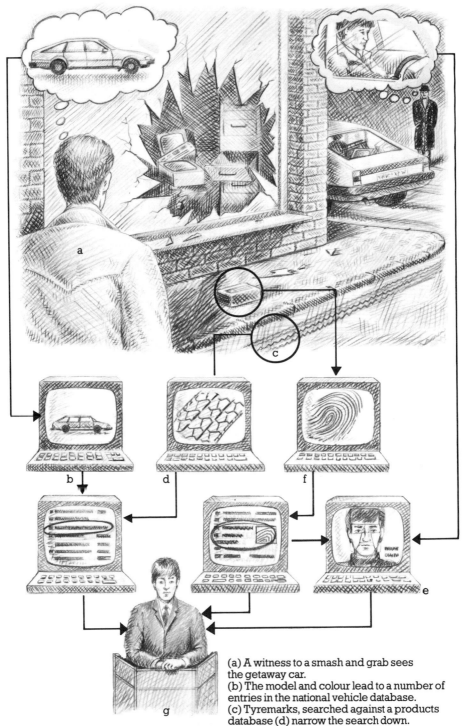

(a) A witness to a smash and grab sees the getaway car.

(b) The model and colour lead to a number of entries in the national vehicle database.

(c) Tyremarks, searched against a products database (d) narrow the search down.

(e) A second witness sees the driver. A photofit produces a description which leads to a small number of known criminals.

(f) Incomplete fingerprints on the brick used to break the window lead to a small number of entries in Criminal Records.

(g) The 'intersection' of these three databases points to two or three suspects. The criminal is soon arrested.

3.4 Searching the database

How do people search databases? They type in a name and get an address. They knew the name precisely and the database finds it for them. One might call this an 'exact match'. They type in a town and get a list of people who live there.

However, very often you do not know exactly where to start. You need to do some sort of 'fuzzy' matching. You know that the person you want lives in a 'Crescent' so you type '*Cresc*' into the address field. Why would you do that, you wonder? Because it is almost a software convention that '*' means 'match any amount of text' and 'Crescent' may have been abbreviated to 'Cresc'. This search command will match 'Mornington *Crescent*' or 'Juniper *Cresc.*' but also, unfortunately, '*Cresc*endo Gardens'. You have to be careful about your questions. Even if you are careful, a database can often surprise you.

If you are going to Reading and you want to pull out all your customers who live there so you can visit them, you could type 'RG*' into the post code field and so match 'RG3 7QT' or 'RG0 1BB3'. If you were an American and wanted to mail everyone you knew in Montana, you would search with 'MO*' as the zip code.

The same technique allows one to search for a word, or a string of words, in a piece of text. For instance, a search in an employment agency database for someone who ought not to be sent to an Arab country might use the command '*drink*' in the remarks field. This would match to the comment 'An agreeable man, but unfortunately a heavy **drink**er in his spare time'.

A less often used variant of this is the ability to search for a fixed number of unknown characters. You might, for instance, want first names like 'Tom', 'Tim', 'Tan'. You should be able to search for them with some command like 'T??', where each ?, by convention, means a single, unspecified character. You have a database of engine parts with numbers like DKE326. You know that all diesel engine parts begin with a D, that all exhaust system parts have E in the third position. So, to find all diesel exhaust system parts you look for D?E???.

In the Superfile system there is also a phonetic search. You can look for names that, when written out, sound like the one you want – like 'Smythe' for 'Smith'. This is a useful feature for computer users who deal with the public over the telephone or face to face. Legend has it that the method, or 'algorithm' as we like to say in the trade, was invented by the resourceful Mr Hollerith of punched card fame, for the American Census of 1890. The Census Bureau was faced with large numbers of people with unpronounceable handles. Many Mr Brodzwyckis had emigrated to the golden shore and neither they nor anyone else had the faintest idea how to spell their names.

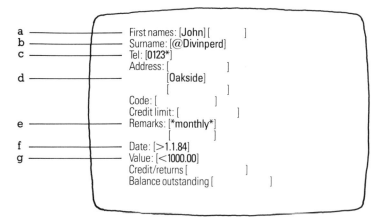

a — First names: [John] [   ]
b — Surname: [@Divinperd]
c — Tel: [0123*]
   Address: [   ]
d —   [Oakside]
           [   ]
   Code: [   ]
   Credit limit: [   ]
e — Remarks: [*monthly*]
           [   ]
f — Date: [>1.1.84]
g — Value: [<1000.00]
   Credit/returns [   ]
   Balance outstanding [   ]

(a) Look for 'John' in the first field
(b) Look for anyone whose name sounds like 'Divinperd'
(c) Look for anyone on the 0123 exchange ('*'matches any further entry)
(d) Look for everyone in 'Oakside' without knowing into which field the word
    was originally entered
(e) Look for anyone with the word 'monthly' in their Remarks field
(f) Look for anyone with an invoice date later than 1.1.84
(g) Look for anyone who bought something costing less than £1000

'Fuzzy' searching in a Superfile database for items that are not precisely known.

The algorithm is now known as 'Soundex' (Knuth, 1973) and works in the following manner:

(1) The initial letter of the word is kept.
(2) Each vowel, 'h', 'y' and doubled consonant is removed.
(3) The remaining consonants are classified into six groups with similar sounds: 'b', 'v', 'd' for instance, sound the same and are coded by the same number.

The upshot of this is that, for instance, 'Smythe', codes as 'S12' – assuming that 'm' = 1 and 't'= 2. Since this is the same as 'Smith' , the object has been achieved of finding names that sound like 'Smith'.

In Spanish, which pronounces words exactly as they are spelled, this would probably work perfectly. English is more difficult. 'Tomson' and 'Thompson' sound the same and should be found by Soundex – but will not because of the 'p'. It would be possible to modify Soundex to treat 'mp' as 'm' (as it treats 'ck' as 'k'), but what about 'preamplifier' where the 'p' *is* pronounced? And further, what about 'Cholmondeley' (pronounced 'Chumley') and 'Cockburn' (pronounced 'Coburn')?

The other sort of thing a database holds is numbers. You might want to find someone who owes you £43.56, but it is much more likely that you want to search for all the people with debts greater than £1000. And this should be easy with '> 1000' in the debt field.

This leads to a subtler but even more important problem. It often happens that we want to store lists of qualities in a record. For instance, in Britain, addresses tend to be rather vague things. They may be just a name and a town as:

Address 1	American Express
Address 2	BRIGHTON

Or they can run to half a dozen lines:

Address 1	The Dower House
Address 2	The Manor
Address 3	Gilded Lane
Address 4	Smart Crescent
Address 5	Jewelled Heights
Address 6	BRIGHTON

The problem here is that when you look, say, for people who live in Brighton, you do not know whether to look for that word in the second address field or the sixth or any one in between.

Americans and Europeans will say, rather smugly, that this is of no importance to them because they have their addresses properly organized into three standard lines:

Address 1	1140 Winter Heights
Address 2	Lawrenceville
Address 3	MO 2345

But let us not think that they can escape so easily from all these problems. What do they do about companies and their directors? We might want to find all the companies that Mr Johnson is a director of:

Company	Small Business Inc.	Mega Galactic Inc.
Director 1	Smith	Andrews
Director 2	*Johnson*	Schultz
Director 3		Creasey
Director 4		Donovan
...		...
Director 54		*Johnson*

The same problem arises very acutely in document storage systems – which will get more and more popular as large capacity Winchester and laser disks become available. Here it often happens that a set of reference words are stored with the document. In a medical system you might have these words describing a paper about injuries: 'leg', 'fracture', 'contusion', 'emergency treatment'. The user of the database might want to look up a paper about 'contusions' and 'legs'... He or she does not expect to have to know where, in the list of key words for the required paper each of these words will occur or even what order these words appear in. If the user feels like typing in 'contusions' first and then 'legs' the system should find a document in whose key word list 'legs' comes before 'contusions'.

On paper this may seem a rather academic problem: in front of the computer it is very real.

A photographer keeps details of photos under ten possible key words. He comes back from an expedition to Sri Lanka with a beautiful picture which he files under the key words: sunset, nets, boats, fishermen, Indian Ocean – in that order. Months later, a magazine rings up and asks to buy a picture of native fishermen coming home in the evening. Unless he has phenomenally accurate memory (in which case he will not need a database manager anyway) he is most unlikely to remember that 'fishermen' was the fourth key word and that 'sunset' was the first.

There may be other ways of coping with this, but I have not come across them. The Superfile system treats lists of items in a record as being logically equivalent. You can store all the items in a person's address under the single descriptor, or tag, ADDRESS, and then ask for 'ADDRESS = Pasadena'. You could ask for 'DIRECTOR = Johnson' or 'INJURY = leg' or 'SUBJECT = sunset'.

In more conventional systems you would have to ask something clumsy like 'IF DIRECTOR 1 = Johnson OR DIRECTOR 2 = Johnson OR DIRECTOR 3 = Johnson OR . . . '. Which would not be very satisfactry on two counts: (1) it would be very tedious to type in; and (2) until you have searched the database, there is no way of knowing how many ORs to include.

You should be able to combine the searches mentioned so far into logical formulae. This is called 'logical' or 'Boolean' searching (after George Boole, the mathematician who first formalized symbolic logic). You can combine the searches mentioned above to produce the effect of: 'If the word "drink" appears *and* he owes more than £1000 *or* he is in the SW postal districts *and* owes less than £300'. Of course, since computers do not yet speak English, you will have to tell the system what you want using computer readable symbols.

There is a hidden joke in searching. You have to know what it is you are looking for. This sounds obvious, but it has some tricky implications. There are many names of things in common use that people spell or abbreviate differently each time they use them. For example, the names of British counties: 'Hertfordshire' or 'Herts.'? 'Buckinghamshire' should be abbreviated 'Bucks.' but I have seen it as 'Bckms.'. 'Shropshire' is properly abbreviated as 'Salop' (the short version of its Latin name) , but very few people know that now – they call it 'Shrops.'. Your company may have some salespersons (John, Mary, Harry, Bill...) who are identified on customer records (so that they get their commissions) by their first names. Bill would be most vexed if half his sales went in under 'William' – who then got his percentage.

The only answer is to control what goes in so that if it is decided that 'Bucks.' is the proper usage, the database manager will not accept 'Buckinghamshire' or 'Bckms.', and you have a fighting chance of finding what you want. A good database manager must have facilities for checking what users type in against a list of acceptable entries. And this means that the person who sets up the database must think out all this sort of thing before work starts.

3.5 Deleting records

The main job of a database manager is very simple. It stores records, finds them, deletes and alters them. This last produces most of the problems. One of the virtues of a fixed Record system is that the new Record is just the same length as the old one, so it can be written in the same space. In a variable length Record system this is almost certain not to be true, so an altered record is just the original one deleted, changed and added again. The trouble with alteration is that – life being what it is – people very often delete things and then wish they had not. We coped with this all too human trait in Superfile by making deletion a two stage process: the first time round the original record stays where it is, but is marked internally as deleted and can be retrieved by a special set of commands. The second time round, a process called 'tidying' or 'garbage collection' in more conventional computer language, is applied to the database, which physically removes the old records and shifts the remaining ones up to use the space (an operating system has the same problem but much worse. See Chapter 1). Of course, the process of shifting records up makes nonsense of the indexes, so a new set has to be created at the same time.

3.6 Reports

One handy way of dividing up database operations is to say that when records are entered, looked at, altered and erased, they are dealt with one by one through the screen forms utility. When users want to deal with records in bulk – to total up their sales for January, to write a standard letter to all their overdue debtors, or to produce a printed list of books on disestablishmentarianism – they use a report generator.

A report generator is similar to a forms generator in that it drags records out of the database according to some predetermined criteria and presents them neatly shaped to the user. Of course, instead of presenting them one by one on the screen, they appear one after the other on a sheet of paper through the computer's printer. Because a report is about *tables* of

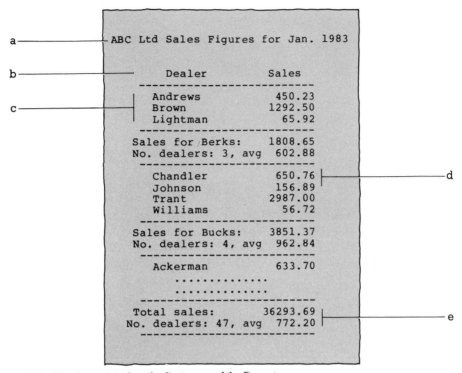

```
a ─────────── ABC Ltd Sales Figures for Jan. 1983


b ─────────            Dealer          Sales
                 -------------------------------
                   Andrews           450.23
c ─────────────┤   Brown            1292.50
                   Lightman           65.92
                 -------------------------------
                 Sales for Berks:   1808.65
                 No. dealers: 3, avg  602.88
                 -------------------------------
                   Chandler          650.76 ├──────── d
                   Johnson           156.89
                   Trant            2987.00
                   Williams           56.72
                 -------------------------------
                 Sales for Bucks:   3851.37
                 No. dealers: 4, avg  962.84
                 -------------------------------
                   Ackerman          633.70
                    . . . . . . . . . . . . . .
                    . . . . . . . . . . . . . .
                 -------------------------------
                 Total sales:      36293.69 ├──────── e
                 No. dealers: 47, avg 772.20
                 -------------------------------
```

(a) Main Header, printed on the first page of the Report.
(b) Page Header, incorporating a page count.
(c) Report lines, containing names sorted alphabetically, and a sales figure.
(d) Sub total lines, printed when a selected field (County) changes – in this case, from 'Berks' to 'Bucks'.
(e) Main total lines, repeating the functions of the subtotals for the whole Report.

The elements of a Superfile Report. It consists of five main parts, shown above, and is a print-out in columns of selected Values from the database. They can be sorted, totalled and calculated.

information, the syllable 'tab' is often found in the trade names of report generators, e.g. 'Filetab', 'Supertab'.

As with forms definition, a report will be set out by someone who understands a bit about computers and how the enterprise's operations work, and it may be used by someone quite different who knows little about computers and cares less. People have different ideas about reports – these are mine:

A report consists of five things:

(1) A main header which goes on the first page and explains what the document is about. When the pre-defined report is run, the user should be able to type in a few fields to date this particular run, note who was responsible for producing it etc.

(2) There need to be page headers which explain what the columns in the report mean.

(3)   The meat of the whole operation is in the report line(s) which consists of pre-set fields into which items are dragged from the database. In the report on page 71 there is only one report line; if you were printing names and addresses, there might be five or six. The report generator should be capable of doing calculations in the report line – just as the forms package could.

(4) If the report has previously been sorted on certain fields, so as to bring, say, all one's dealers in different American states together, then it would be possible to throw a sub-total when the State changes from 'Kansas' to 'Mississippi'. The sub-total line should be able to add up various fields in the report since the last sub-total. It should be able to count how many records there were and to calculate averages and things like that.

(5) Finally, at the bottom of the whole report there will probably be a total which does the work of the sub-totals but over all the information printed.

It makes a report generator much more useful if it is possible to have the form that created the data in the first place on the screen so that the user can put search controls into it. One might, for instance, only want a report on the dealers who had sold more than £10 000 worth of goods.

3.7 Programming around the database

The database package at the core of a database manager consists of two parts: the underlying slave into whose hands you put documents for filing and from whom you get them back; and the programming language that lets you do useful things with it all – the method of controlling the slave.

To date the most widely used database package for micros has been *dBASE II*. It consists of an invisible scheme for indexing, storing and finding records, and a language 'D', in which the user writes programs to make the database fit into real life.

Of course, the database packages we see on microcomputers are the primitive descendants of many years of database management on mainframe machines. A voluminous and almost impenetrable literature has grown up around the subject, and a number of very expensive packages have been written to do the multitude of finnicky jobs that accumulate round data. Another problem with traditional database management has been the effect of over-professionalization. Until very recently, databases were administered by computer professionals who made their livings, not to put too fine a point on it, by making a mystery of the whole business. In a company like a bank, where the database of clients *was* the business, the computer people had great status. Unfortunately, professional groups with no outside forces to battle against, tend to take off into a spiral of technical mysteries.

A great deal of database literature is to do with mathematical concepts which seem to have been invented just to make a showring where programmers can exhibit their skills. A recent review of database managers for DEC's VAX machines criticized pretty well all of them for breaking 'the first normal form by supporting repeating data groups'. A repeating data group is the very useful feature we saw in ADDRESS in Chapter 2. It might well be worth breaking the first normal form in order to have it; but it seems that professional database management has drifted off into a heaven of pure theory where usefulness to the customer is not a relevant consideration.

The trouble with database work is that it is very unpredictable. If you sit down at your micro to do word processing you are dealing with pretty standard sort of stuff: letters, words, paragraphs, chapters and so on. The designers of word processing software can draw on the traditions of European literacy established over two thousand years to predict what you will want to do. Spread sheet calculators too are very predictable things: although not very easy to write, the author has a good idea, based on 500 years of accounting of what the user may want to do. Unhappily, there are almost as many designs of database as there are enterprises that use them. One user wants a list of customers and their purchases. Another wants to store movements of a robot's arm and the inputs to the six motors necessary to achieve them. A third has a database of Himalayan mountains, the access passes, the legal formalities necessary to get up them. A fourth keeps records of projects and people in the film industry and wants to be able to find all the people who worked on three or more films that grossed more than £50 million. A fifth keeps a database of world events and needs to be able to list all events in the Middle East involving 'oil' and 'explosions' and to be able to trace back to the events that preceded them.

Many of the difficulties that these databases pose are common; many more, unfortunately, are unique to each application. This poses rather a problem for the author of a database package who can only anticipate so much: after that it is up the users to write their own programs to do the clever bits. We postpone the account of enquiry languages to Chapter 5.

3.7 Text databases

As is happening more and more in microcomputing, people are discovering needs which were never addressed by the mainframe world. One of them is text databases and people need these in many different fields. Examples occur wherever data is mixed with text: in medical

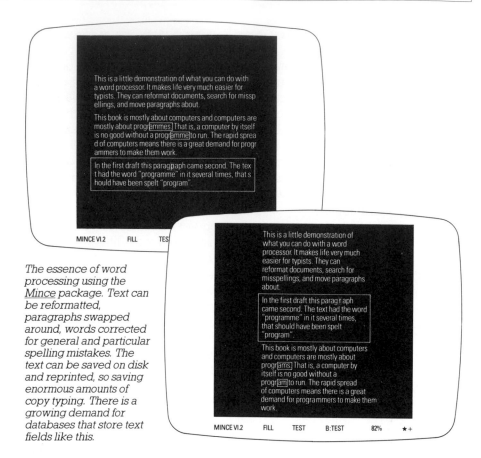

The essence of word processing using the Mince *package. Text can be reformatted, paragraphs swapped around, words corrected for general and particular spelling mistakes. The text can be saved on disk and reprinted, so saving enormous amounts of copy typing. There is a growing demand for databases that store text fields like this.*

reports; surveys, prototype tests etc. An interesting application is in bibliography.

Each Record in such a database has a number of conventional elements: citation number; title; author(s); publisher or source and a date; the number of pages; the number of references; digest.

These might not be terribly easy to handle in a fixed Record database because they all vary in size. But what makes it completely different is the last bit, the digest. This lump of text may range from 0 characters to about 1000. The user needs full word processing to enter and edit it and the database manager *must* have variable length Records if it is to store the text efficiently.

What is wanted for this application is a blend between word processing and database management. Since there is no other package, so far as I know, that can cope, I will have to describe how we have provided for these needs in Superfile by incorporating the code for an excellent word processing package called variously *Mince**, *The Final Word* and *Perfectwriter* – all written by a firm called Mark of the Unicorn Inc.

Mince was an excellent foundation for this enhancement because it already provided two windows on the screen and the facility for editing seven different documents at once – displaying pairs of them together in the screen windows. What we did was to integrate Mince with our existing forms package so that the word processing screen was reduced to the contents of fields. In other words, the user could move the cursor about the screen in the usual word-processing way, but only within the fields provided by the form.

In order to cope with variable length items we made the fields 'soft' – they started out only one character wide and expanded to contain whatever the user typed in. In many cases the fields ended up looking much as they would in a fixed field form because the data typed into them was of fairly standard length. However, fields that contained items like the digest (above) could expand to accept as much text as the user wanted.

The repeated field feature – which makes it possible to deal with lists of qualities in a Record – was so useful in earlier versions of Superfile, that we incorporated it into this version too. A special character would exit the field in which text was being entered and create a new one with the same tag.

We had to tackle two further problems in order to produce a useful free text database manager. The whole point of a database is to be able to *find* records quickly by searching on anything within them. Searches on small fields presented no new problem, but often people would be searching for key words in big text fields. This could be done by the usual search for a particular portion of text in a larger, unknown piece†. But this would be slow since the database manager would have to look at every word of text stored under the appropriate tag. To simplify this the database manager might provide a way for the user to skip through the completed text, positioning the cursor on key words and pulling them out into a set of key word fields by pressing a control character.

Finally we had to improve our sorting package so that it could cope with repeated tags – like key words or multiple authors – producing an entry in the sorted database for each item under a repeated tag. So for instance, if a book written by Brown, Smith and Jones called 'Massive Mountains' were part of a bibliographic database, one would expect to find three entries in a print-out sorted by author:

Brown, Smith, Jones; *Massive Mountains*
Jones, Brown, Smith; *Massive Mountains*
Smith, Brown, Jones; *Massive Mountains*

*Mince is based on a mainframe word processor at Massachussetts Institute of Technology called EMACS. The name 'Mince' is an acronym for 'Mince Is Not Complete EMACS' – an example of the unfortunate passion programmers have for recursive jokes.

†If you want to search for the word 'gnats', which you expect to find in the middle of some other text like: 'When night fell the attentions of the gnats became unbearable.', the convention is that you search for '*gnats*'. The asterisks mean 'any text'.

3.9 Picture databases

Now that business micros have reasonably high definition screens and printers can draw quite nice pictures, there is no reason why we should not have combined picture and text databases.

A picture would be stored in the database as a string of bytes which are interpreted in a form as a special kind of field. The screen forms generator has code in it which recognizes a picture field and 'draws' the bytes.

A picture is drawn on the computer screen in a very simple-minded way. The screen is composed of small areas which can be white, black, or some tone in between depending on the values of the data bytes associated with them. These areas are called 'pixels'. In a colour system a pixel can also have one of the three primary colours. A picture is made up of a large number of pixels culled from a file – or, in this case, from the database Record. So far as I know, no one has produced a package that does this, but – given suitable hardware – there seems no great difficulty about it.

A Record with a picture in it might look like this:

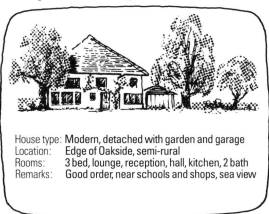

```
House type: Modern, detached with garden and garage
Location:   Edge of Oakside, semi-rural
Rooms:      3 bed, lounge, reception, hall, kitchen, 2 bath
Remarks:    Good order, near schools and shops, sea view
```

Hardware advances will soon allow pictures to be stored in databases alongside text. Here, a house agent's stock in trade.

A picture like this is a chunk of data bytes with no manipulable structure in it. Things get more interesting when pictures have some structure. A simple example would be a database that knew about photofit pictures for identification of criminal suspects. A witness might say that the wanted man had chinese eyes, a bald head, wide cheek-bones, a moustache etc. These elements are held in the database, when assembled they make a picture, but they also produce a piece of text that 'describes' the appearance of the criminal. It should then be possible for the database manager to search its criminal records to find people whose faces have the same classification.

A dentist might keep dental records for his patients. His database

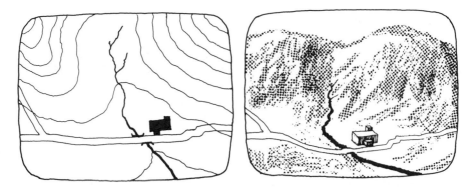

A map can be stored as a database and displayed (left) in the conventional way; (right) as the pilot of an aircraft might see the scene.

manager would know about buccal crowns and canines and store the data about the ironwork in a usable form. More important, if the dentist did a filling in a molar, the system should put the appropriate symbol in the right place and store a corresponding text item in the database Record.

Maps present another great opportunity. If you open an atlas at the front you see maps; if you open it at the back you find a gazetteer – a list of places with some description and the latitude and longitude. A gazetteer in a database, when run through a not very complicated piece of software, should produce the original map. Add populations, rivers, hills, railways, roads and coastlines and you have something that people in the distribution and service industries would find very useful.

The original map is an idealized version of the surface of the Earth seen from a long way away. There is no reason why the same information should not be presented in picture form as what you would see from closer up – say from an aeroplane over a certain position at a height of 300 feet looking north. The USAF – that treasure house of high tech toys – is working on hardware to present its aeronautical charts in just this manner. And, of course, once a map is held in a database it can be updated in real time. Again, in the USAF's case, it would be updated with intelligence of anti-aircraft defences, targets and ex-targets.

3.10 Spread sheet packages

Another useful combination of existing software packages would be a database manager with a spread sheet. A spread sheet, for those who are lucky enough not to have had to wrestle with the object, is a computerized version of the accountant's rows and columns layout.

It could be said that spread sheet computing first launched the micro as a serious office tool. The *Visicalc* package was the first real software success

Joe Soap Inc.				
Quarters:	1	2	3	4
EXPENSES				
Employees	9	10	11	12
- - - -	- - -	- - -	- - -	- - -
Wages	63000	68600	74760	81536
Overheads	36000	39200	42720	46592
Materials	40000	44000	48400	53240
P & P	8000	8800	9680	10648
- - - -	- - -	- - -	- - -	- - -
Total Paid	147000	160600	175560	192016
====	===	===	===	===
Units Sold	8000	8800	9680	10648
- - - -	- - -	- - -	- - -	- - -
INCOME				
Sales	152000	167200	183920	202312
====	===	===	===	===
Quarterly movt.	5000	6600	8360	10296
Bank Balance	−20000	−15000	−8400	−40

Spread sheets are perhaps the most popular software packages to be used on micros so far. In a sense they are databases, in which the rows are items and the columns Records.

story, and it is said that it was responsible for Apple's vast sales back in the early 1980s.

A spread sheet consists of rows and columns of figures, though it is possible to have text entries (usually in the top row and the left hand column) and rows of dashes to show where totals are calculated. The figures in the sheet can either be entered directly or can be calculated by formulae built in by the person who set it up, from other figures. Thus a cash flow for a widget factory may have built into it the fact that every three employees can make 100 widgets a week. Their wages and overheads follow automatically. The revenue from selling the widgets can be calculated from their sale price: the profit of the enterprise is income less costs. Given all these relationships, the manager can experiment with different rates of production to see what produces the best profit.

An ordinary spread sheet expects you to type in the figures needed in the various slots. However, a computerized business will almost certainly have the figures in its database. To see them in spread sheet form – which can be very useful – they need to be extracted. A spread sheet is therefore another form of front end for a database manager.

And, of course, it is not a very exotic form of presentation. If you think of a database as rows (items) arranged in columns (Records) you immediately have a spread sheet. At any one moment you want to look at part of the layout, with totals brought in to show the effect of previous events.

		Records		
	Jan	Feb	Mar	Apr
Wages	2300	2300	2400	2400
Overheads	1600	1600	1700	1700
Advertising	2000	2000	1800	1800

Items

Life being what it is, things are not actually that simple because the *actual* Records will be more detailed than shown here. 'Wages' in 'Feb' (2300) is the total of lots of payments to individual employees during that month. Overheads is the total of a whole lot of other things like rent, rates, light, heat etc. entered as single transaction Records in the database. So the extraction of data from a database for presentation in a spread sheet may not be as simple as it might seem at first sight. Moreover, the 'Records' extracted may be 'virtual' Records, made up from other, scattered Records in a relational database. (See Chapter 4.)

I may be maligning someone, but so far I have not seen any software that does this well. There are things like *Lotus 1 2 3, The incredible Jack* and *T-Maker*, which purport to do some of these things with word processing thrown in, but to my mind they are not satisfactory. The presentation is slick, but they are not really database managers in the sense that they cannot handle big databases fast and make up virtual Records out of different Record types.

We will have to wait for advances in the art of guessing what standard operations enough end users want before we can write configurable software for them. For, remember, if there were only one customer with enough money, wanting this kind of software, it would be easy enough to write a program for him or her. What is difficult is writing a program that many people with a modest amount of knowledge and money can shape into the specific programs they actually want.

3.11 Graphics

There is a school of thought that says that numbers, the raw material of almost all business operations, are meaningless and that the only thing the businessman can understand is graphs – and the more prettily coloured they are the better. If they can be made to look three dimensional with shadows he will be in ecstasies. I suspect that much of the impetus behind this is the passionate desire felt by the hardware manufacturers to make their machines look different from other functionally identical machines. It is quite noticeable that at exhibitions the punters (an ignoble term, but there is really none better for the open-mouthed computer neophytes) cluster round any stand on which a terminal is drawing things in colour. It does not matter what it is drawing in colour so long as the colours are there – as thick, bright and meaningless as a nursery school finger painting. A favourite demonstration is an isometric drawing of a three dimensional graph of some fairly simple mathematical function. Physicists rightly use this device to present difficult mathematical ideas: the technique has no place in business and hardly one businessman in a million will have any idea what he is looking at. All he can see is that it looks very high tech and impressive.

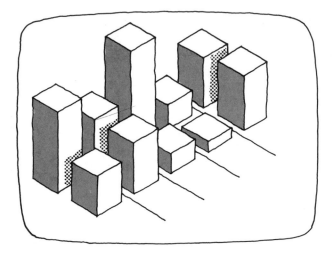

People who buy computers seem to insist that they draw bar charts. But are they any use?

Vast effort is therefore invested to make computers produce bar and pie charts on their screens and printers. Behind the physical devices there has to go rather elaborate software to take tables of numbers, from a spread sheet or a database and turn them into these pictures.

Month	Jan	Feb	Mar	Apr	May	Jun
Sales	12	14	23	26	18	10

The same problem arises in extracting these numbers from the database as arises with the spread sheet. The sales totals here may be made up of many individual transactions which have to be totalled with some sort of software like a report generator, but one that is run several times to produce sales totals for each month. Then, in order to draw a graph, the software must run through the list, work out the greatest and least values, scale all the values so that the graph fills up the page nicely, and plot the points. It is not easy to imagine an easy way of presenting software that can be configured to do these tasks in a multitude of different situations.

Alternatively, the person in charge might think that a pie chart would look better. The software has to total the numbers involved, and divide 360° into the same proportions.

Not the least of the drawbacks to the whole thing lies in the various untruthful methods that can be used to make graphs look different. If we plot this graph with 10 as the smallest sale shown (graph a), then the ups and downs look quite alarming. If we take zero as the smallest (graph b), then the variation is less impressing. If we use a logarithmic scale on the y axis (graph c) everything gets even more flattened out.

These tricks are well known to people who deal in graphs; it may not be so wise to let a machine apply them indiscriminately.

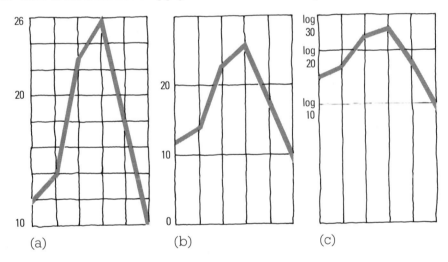

(a) (b) (c)

CHAPTER FOUR

MULTI-FILE DATABASES

So far we have assumed, because it makes things easier to explain, that a single database contains only Records of the same shape. In a real computer system there will almost certainly be Records of several different shapes which hang together in more or less complicated ways, making several databases or several 'files' (terminology varies. See Section 1.2 for an explanation of computer files).

To make things clear each of these things is often called a 'logical database', a 'flat file', or a 'logical file'. This distinction is necessary in, say, the Superfile system (see Chapter 2) where all the data is held in a single physical data file.

For instance, the name and address of a customer is one sort of Record; information about any transactions with you is another, data about purchases is a third and data about the manufacturer of those purchases is a fourth.

In a library system, the title, author, publisher, shelf number etc. of a book could be one Record; names and dates of borrowers another. In a database of companies, one sort of Record would be information about a company's organization; another its annual returns.

An airline might have a database consisting of Records describing: its aeroplanes; its staff's names, addresses, qualifications etc.; the planned services; the actual flights (which aircraft, which crew, where the plane actually was, and the passengers on the flight).

In all these examples, Records were linked in some way with Records of different types. This need not necessarily be so: a database of political and economic events needs to have each event linked to others of the same sort. An oil company announces an oil strike in a part of the world hitherto considered to be wasteland. Some months later the government there buys itself an airline and a year later several London and New York merchant banks open branch offices in the capital. Each Record produces a cascade of ensuing Records.

A Record consists of various bits of information that need to go together. One of the big theoretical difficulties about database work is that there is no simple recipe for determining what items of data should go in one sort of Record and what in another. It is usually quite obvious when you think about it, but just what goes where is left to the common sense of the person who set up the system. Normally, one groups together data that will not change very often. For instance people usually stay at one address for quite a long time. In many databases it makes sense to keep names and addresses in a single Record. However, a database which kept track of a company's sales reps,

*An airline will keep a number of databases to keep track of its working materials:
flights, staff, aircraft, services and passengers.*

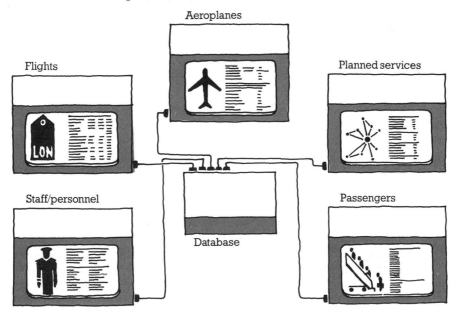

who were often moving from one hotel to another, might keep the salesperson's name and home address in one Record and his or her current hotel address in another. The two are linked to show where each salesperson is at any particular moment. To take the idea further, there might be only a few hundred hotels that were ever used by the sales team, and it might be handy to keep them all in the database all the time, with some mechanism to show which hotel each salesperson was staying in on a particular night. Just how this mechanism might work is what makes databases interesting.

The simple-minded solution to the multi-Record problem is just to keep all the data in every Record. So, for instance, the airline's database might have a file of huge Records that have in them each aircraft, its engineering history, the names and addresses of its crew, the names of all the passengers, its cargo, where it is etc. Whenever a new flight started, this mass of material would have to be copied into the new Record.

In the business database, each invoice would have to record the customer's name and address, the date of the transaction, what was bought, where it was bought from, our stockholding of that item etc. This mass of information would often be irrelevant to the particular job in hand, if that job were, for instance, producing an invoice.

This approach means storing the same piece of information many times over – for instance, each customer's full name and address and details of his credit-worthiness etc. are stored in every transaction Record. This is cumbersome, slows up every operation and wastes a lot of expensive disk space. But worse than that it is functionally inept. If our customer changes address, we have to go through the database and change all the Records. Suppose we want to keep the old address as well? We have to keep one or more transactions that mention the old address. The whole principle of database work is that you should have a *single*, easily accessible source for each piece of information.

Happily, many real-life stores of information do result in a flat file database, consisting of a single Record type. But, there are also many applications which cannot be crammed into this format, and the best solution then is to store the database in lots of small Records that are automatically linked together.

How would this linking be done? The obvious way is often the best way, and that is by including a unique common item in the two Records you want to link. Given that everything in the database is indexed, then each of them 'points' to the other: each of them can be found from the other. Of course either of these Records may include items that point to one or more other kinds of Records. Let us look in detail at how this would work for the business database.

Using the Superfile convention of tags and items, each customer has a

Record like this:

XNAME = Mary
SNAME = Smith
ADDRESS = The Larches
ADDRESS = Magnolia St
ADDRESS = Kingston
CUSTID = 34924

Each time she buys something, the system generates a Record like this (CUSTID = 34924 is the linking item):

CUSTID = 34924
DATE = 24 Feb 1984
STOCKLTR = aac
STOCKNUM = 66831

This Record is a bit less clear, but it just says that on a certain date, our customer with the ID number '34924' bought a stock item identified with the letters 'aac' – which might be where we keep it – and the numbers '66831'.

Now the mystery is to know what she bought. What is an 'aac 66831'? The stock Record answers that:

STOCKLTR = aac
STOCKNUM = 66831
DESCRIPTION = 'Hypertronic' electric typewriter
MFGR = Hypoid Typewriter Co.
MFGNUM = PL34251
SERIAL = 229221
PRICE = 221.67

This Record tells us that the object with the stock letter and number in the sales Record is in fact a Hypertronic electric typewriter, made by Hypoid. We know its manufacturer's type number and this machines serial number and, most important, how much it costs.

Another Record details our order to the wholesaler for a dozen of these machines – one of which has now been sold:

DATE = 1 Nov 1983
STOCKNUM = 66831
SUPPLID = 4545
PRICE = 1862.03
QUANTITY = 12

And finally, we have a name and address Record for the wholesaler:

COMPANY = Stellar Stationery Wholesale
ADDRESS = PO Box 2
ADDRESS = New York
SUPPLID = 4545

A relational database with these four Record types might look like this if you spread everything out:

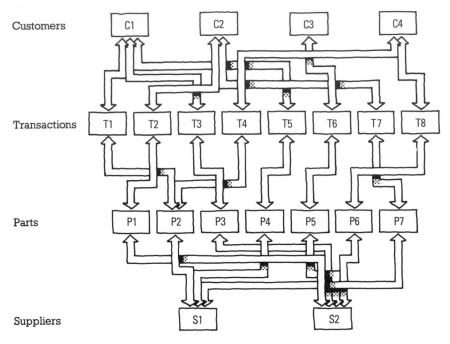

In a relational database, Records point to each other so that essential data is only held once. Here is the database for a business with customer, transaction, parts and supplier Records.

We are now in a position to answer pretty well any question about our business. We can combine the relevant bits of these Records to make an invoice. We can pull out other bits to make up our accounts. If it turns out that a batch of these typewriters with serial numbers between 229200 and 229300 were built with potentially dangerous carriage return keys, we can easily search our database for transactions involving these machines and write to the people who bought them. If our engineer is going to Kingston for the day, we can find all the people on whom to call.

What does such a search entail? We start with what we know, which is that the DESCRIPTION includes the word 'Hypertronic' and 229200 ‹SERIAL ‹229300 (that is, the serial number is greater than 229200 and less than 229300). That will find us the stock Record(s). From that we can get the stock letters and number: STOCKLTR = aac, STOCKNUM = 66831. If we search with that we can find all the transactions in which people bought this machine – among them the customer with CUSTID = 34924. We search again with that and the condition that ADDRESS = Kingston for each CUSTID. We find Ms Smith, among others.

In conventional databases there are definite Record types. A customer's name and address Record is one, and the transactions another. These types are fixed, so the system knows what fields they contain. In such a case, the software running the relational search just needs to know what type of Record to look for next, and something in it. In Superfile there are no fixed Record types – any Record may have more or less fields than its prototype. So each time we do one of these searches using data out of the preceding Record, we steer the search towards the Record we want by mentioning a tag that only occurs in the second Record. For instance, if we just go to the database and ask for Records with CUSTID = 34924, we will find *both* Mary Smith's customer Record *and* all her transaction Records. In this case we just want the customer Record so we can find that address, so we search with the fuller model:

CUSTID = 34924
SNAME =

Since the transactions Records do not have the tag SNAME in them, they will not be found. Conversely, if we have the customer ID and want the transactions, we search with:

CUSTID = 34924
DATE =

and it will find them because the address Record does not have a DATE tag in it. This is pretty simple to describe and relatively easy to automate – because, of course, we must remember that the end user does not want to have to remember the tags, CUSTID, DATE, etc. He or she wants to see pieces of information appearing in a form. But this just demands that, as before, we link tags with fields.

4.1 Relational calculus

In the jargon of the trade, this sort of database, where one Record is linked to another by having the contents of certain fields in common, is 'relational'*.

The word 'relation' comes from the 'relational calculus' a branch of set theory in mathematics. What follows is a digression just to get the reader up to date with what other people may be talking about.† The 'ideal',

---

*There are a few people who think that 'relational' means that items are related within a Record – that is, if you ask for one item you get the lot. They are technically quite right but not very helpful, since it is hard to see how else a Record could be made up. The terminology can cause confusion.
†For a clear and readable account of formal database theory see Date (1981).

mathematical, relational database looks like this:

Address records

XNAME	SNAME	ADDRESS1	ADDRESS2	ADDRESS3	CUSTID
Fred	Jones	35	High St	Oldham	24251
Mary	Smith	The Larches	Magnolia St	Kingston	34924

Transaction records

CUSTID	DATE	STOCKLTR	STOCKNUM
34924	24 Feb 1984	aac	66831
22726	16 May 1984	aab	55673
34924	23 Jun 1984	ada	29871

The mathematician sees this as two sets which have a common member – the entries in the CUSTID column. In set theory, sets can have a number of relations – here the *join* of the two sets on CUSTID produces synthetic or virtual Records that look like this:

Mary	Smith	The Larches	Magnolia St	Kingston	34924	24 Feb 1984	aac	66831

that is, the name, address and details of one of Mary Smith's transactions. By joining the stock letter and numbers with other Records we can find out what she bought and then, going on, whom she bought it from.

The items linking two Records together may be unique to that pair or may be repeated elsewhere in the database – as with Mary Smith's CUSTID above. They may be repeated many times. They may link Records of different types or Records of the same type. For instance, consider the news item database described in Chapter 3. There, each news item is linked to previous events and will be linked to future events.

A piece of housekeeping that a good relational database manager will do is to keep track of the links and to verify that they are all in place and that no Records have become 'orphaned'. For instance: we may have customer and transaction Records. A transaction Record only makes sense if it is attached to a customer Record. If its customer Record gets erased, or the CUSTID in it is changed, we have a whole mess of ownerless transactions. One way the database manager can avoid this is to keep a count of the number of links in each direction – a customer Record might point to fifteen transactions, while each of fifteen transactions points to the one customer – and to verify that the counts tally in each direction.

The other mathematical thing people want to do with relational databases is to 'project'. Suppose that we run an office equipment business. We have a database of customers, transactions and parts. We sell typewriters by mail order. We want to find out which typewriters were sold to people living in Walsall. If we select the customers in Walsall, then join them to their transactions and then join those to parts and look at the manufacturer fields, we shall find out. It turns out that we sold only two types: the ever popular Hypertronic, and the IMB. We get a list out that looks like this:

Customer	Typewriter type
Mr Smith	Hypertronic
Mr Jones	Hypertronic
Mr Black	IMB
Mr White	Hypertronic
Mr Allan	IMB
Mrs Akenshaw	IMB

What we want is two Records out at the end; what we have got is a mess of Records – one for each customer. We have to go through a further process of sorting the list by manufacturer, to bring all the Hypertronics together and then all the IMBs like this:

Customer	Typewriter type
Mr Smith	Hypertronic
Mr Jones	Hypertronic
Mr White	Hypertronic
Mr Allan	IMB
Mrs Akenshaw	IMB
Mr Black	IMB

and then to de-duplicate the list on 'Typewriter type', by comparing each entry with the one below and eliminating it if they are the same* so that we end up with: Hypertronic, IMB – which is the list, or projection, we wanted.

Superficially, it seems that regarding Records as sets makes life very simple because much work has been done on set theory and the various operations are well understood – by mathematicians at least.

Unfortunately the relational calculus is another example (so common in

---

*This is another reason why a good database manager has to be able to check to see that entries that are *supposed* to be the same actually are the same.

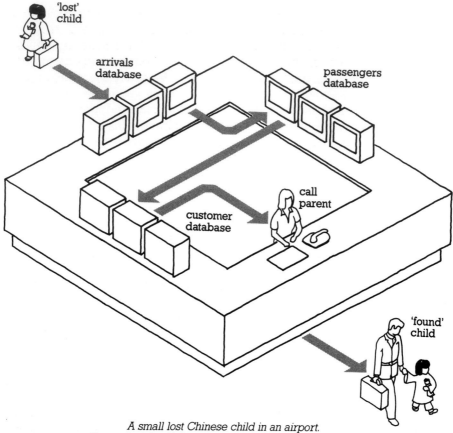

A small lost Chinese child in an airport.
A search of the flight arrivals database shows three flights
from Singapore and Hong-Kong – the most likely departure points. A search
in those flights' passenger lists finds an unaccompanied child of the right age
and sex on one of them. A call to the agent who sold the ticket reveals
the name and address of her father who booked her flight. A call to her home gets
the name of the person who should be meeting her.

the high tech world) of a solution looking for a problem. Real-life data does not fall neatly into the abstractions of sets. The main problem is that a set can contain only one member of each data type. Yet, as we have seen, the idea of the repeated item is a very useful and powerful one that fits in with the way people think and work. Furthermore, ordinary computer users do not think in set theory. The ideas of join or projection, lucid though they may be to mathematicians, do not cause end-users' eyes to sparkle. Any reasonably intelligent computer user can understand in a vague, practical way how common items can link two or more Records together, but it is no use trying to freight that understanding with a lot of theory that is irrelevant to the practical problems in hand.

The unfortunate result of the near similarity of real-life databases to set theory is that Parkinson's Law has produced a complete academic discipline which floats freely in the intellectual void. All it seems to do is to confuse the real issues with masses of difficult and spurious theory. It is excellent for setting examination questions, useless to help real computer users.

I may speak somewhat more bitterly of this than I should, but this anecdote will explain why. We first designed Superfile by the light of ignorance. Not knowing how databases worked, we invented one that seemed to do the useful, sensible things in a straightforward way using the facilities available on the ordinary microcomputer of 1981. When we had finished and potential customers invited us to compare it with existing database managers we found ourselves at a loss. There seemed few points of contact because (it appeared to us) the traditional types had been designed in such complicated and self-frustrating ways that they were very difficult both to make and to use. We could not then understand what the problem was.

Time and experience have illuminated this scene. It is all rooted in history. The first commercial computers stored their long-term data on magnetic tape very much as today's home computers store theirs on audio cassettes. Curiously, the magnetic tape drive, now almost obsolete as a useful piece of computer hardware, has become the standard visual symbol in films, television and cartoons for 'computer'.

Anyone who has tried to use a cassette as a medium for data storage will know that it has two very serious drawbacks: you can only search from one end of the tape to another – there is no random access as there is with disks; and it is very difficult to run the tape forward and stop it at the right place to pick up a particular piece of data. These limitations forced the original designers of database managers to do wonderful juggling acts with tape drives, copying fixed Record files from one to the other, merging, sorting and inserting*; solving (to my simple mind) staggeringly difficult problems like the Tower of Hanoi puzzle.†

As so often, the temporary problems of the medium imposed permanent problems of doctrine. The designers of databases having, with great difficulty, solved the problems of tape drives, failed to notice that their solutions overcame non-existent difficulties when their software was

---

*For a glimpse of the difficulties of handling databases on tape, see Knuth (1973). About a third of its 700 pages are to do with these problems.

†The Tower of Hanoi is that tedious game where you have three pegs on one of which is threaded a set of disks of decreasing size. The problem is to turn the whole pile upside down by moving only one disk at a time and always placing it on a disk larger than it. It often appears in computing texts to illustrate the power of recursive programming.

transferred to the freedom of disks. Many of the difficulties people have with conventional database managers can, in my view, be traced to archaic methods inherited from the old technology.

It is as if the captain of the first steamship insisted on tacking to windward as if he were still under sail because it had taken him a lot of time and trouble to learn the art and he was not going to abandon it now just because it was obsolete. Enough complaining; back to business.

The relational approach is simple to understand but rather difficult to program because if it is to work well, all the linking items in the database have to be indexed so that a search can go either way from any Record to any other Records linked to it.

This kind of searching is potentially the most difficult you can ask a database for: many-to-many: many of one sort of Record that may be linked to many of another sort. By contrast, a hierarchical database is one-to-many: each master Record may have dependants, and they in turn may have dependants but each dependant has only one master. The links are built into the database manager and usually can be searched only one way: from master downwards. This is fine if you can guarantee that you only want to search one way. If, as you might well, you want to find all the defective typewriters in Kingston, forget it.

If you start out with a fully indexed flat file you can build a relational database fairly easily. The difficulty comes in getting enough speed out of the thing when a many-to-many search demands repeated passes through the database to satisfy multiple conditions. In big databases the links are often created explicitly by including pointers in one Record to another so that a relational search does not have to rely on the indexing mechanisms. This is all very well, but it demands that:

(1) You know beforehand just what searches are going to be made – for example, the search for the people in Kingston who had bought defective Hypertronic typewriters.

(2) You have the time available to run up and down the database putting the pointers in beforehand. This is an operation functionally akin to indexing – and equally time consuming.

(3) There is enough room in the database to hold all the pointers.

(4) Once the pointers are in, changes made to the database will not invalidate them. To prevent this happening, big database managers often arrange that when Record B, pointed to by Record A, is deleted, it physically stays in place, but points on in some way to the new version of B. In time this builds up spiders webs of pointers that are fragile and out of date.

Some mainframe databases constructed like this become so complicated that if you want to 'reload' them – that is, clear out all the dead Records and the consequent pointers to pointers to pointers – you have to allow many hours of very skilled programmers' time.

4.2 Hierarchical databases

A simpler but less powerful approach is the 'hierarchical' database. Here each Record has a *single* indexed field – the key field. Dependent Records quote their parent's key field in some way known to the database but invisible to the user (remember: the common items which link Records in a relational database are visible to the user). The indexing is much simpler because it only has to cope with the master Records.

In some ways this is perfectly satisfactory. Many data operations on paper take a hierarchical form: a patient is admitted to hospital, a master Record is created to show his name, home address, date of admission, responsible doctor and ward. He then visits the X-ray department a few times. He is prescribed drugs. He goes to physiotherapy. Pathology do some tests on his juices. If things turn out badly, he becomes a Record in the mortuary. All

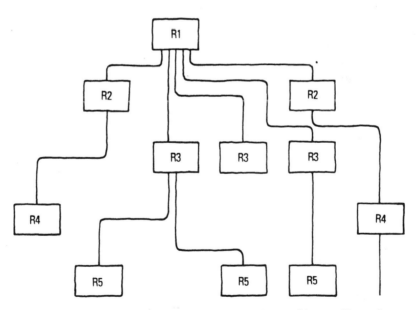

In a hierarchial database 'dependent' Records hang off 'master' Records. This structure can be repeated so that here R1 is the grand master. R2 and R3 hang off it. R4 hangs off R2 and R5 hangs off R3. Of course, each type may be repeated many times.

this fits well into a hierarchical scheme, generating sub-Records of different types that hang off the master Record.

This produces a tree structured database:

This is all very well until you want to find all the patients who were given shots from a defective batch of penicillin. In the relational database you just search for that batch number and then on the patient ID numbers that lead to the patients who were given it. In the hierarchical database you cannot do that. You have to look at every patient, scan down the tree that leads from him or her and see if it leads to a pharmacy Record with the defective batch number. The amount of processing needed is far higher than in the relational scheme.

But there is worse to come. The defects of the hierarchical scheme show up very clearly if we redraw the diagram of a relational database above in an hierarchical form:

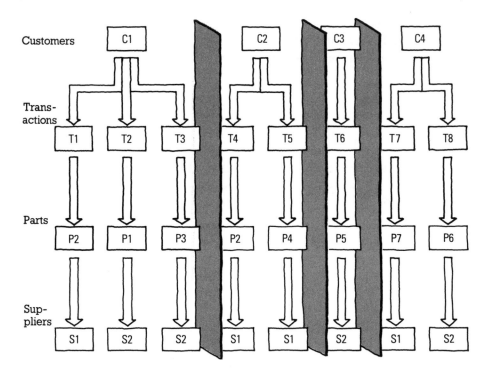

In this case the requirement that every dependent Record hangs off a single parent causes no problems at the first two levels. The customers are the masters and their transactions are dependent. But what about the part Records which show what they have bought? Since several customers may buy the same part in different transactions we find that the hierarchical scheme can force us to have multiple part Records – e.g. part 2 here, which occurs twice because it was sold in transactions 1 and 4. Things get much worse at the supplier level, where our two suppliers, who should be represented by one Record each, in fact both occur four times. This is not only very wasteful of disk space, it also makes maintenance of the database almost impossible: if one of the suppliers changes address, we have to go through the database changing an unknown number of Records.

Another big drawback to the hierarchical database is that we cannot easily hold a supplier who has not yet sold us anything. To do so we would have to hang the supplier off a non-existent customer. Broadly speaking, a hierarchical database is not a very good thing if you can get a relational one. A relational database can always be set up to look like a hierarchical one – but the reverse is not true.

Finally, there is a third scheme called a 'network' database in which the links between records are themselves a type of Record. A Unix software designer once said, 'A network is a great place for losing data.' Hence the insistence in Unix on checkable tree structures to keep files and these files are, in many ways, rather like Records in a database. However, a network database has not yet appeared on a micro, so we shall not trouble ourselves with it.

4.3 Windows

In order to present a multi-file database to the end user we have to put

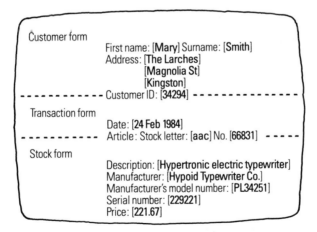

Related Records presented in screen windows. The item, customer ID, links the first two Records; stock letter and number link the second and third. Although a linking item is present in each of the two Records it links, the windowing software automatically only shows it once so it belongs, notionally, to two windows at once.

several forms on the screen at once. The smart idea in microcomputing at the moment is 'windows' – areas of screen which are, in effect, separate screens. In the ordinary implementation of windows, a different program can be running in each area – word processing in one, spread sheet in another, graphs in a third – as if they were separate VDUs connected to three separate processors.

Here we want to run different forms in each window, but to hook them up behind the scenes so that the necessary tags and values are automatically read across from one form to the other to make the relational links. The forms corresponding to individual Records are built, like tiles into a floor, into a super-form. The super-form is told to copy whatever appears in the linking fields in one form to the appropriate fields in another. It may copy a tag and a value, or if no value is given, just the tag so as to direct the search properly. It is easier to draw the process than describe it:

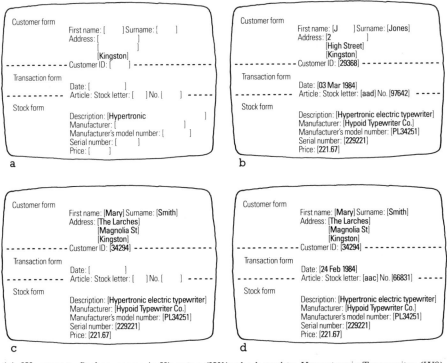

(a) We want to find someone in Kingston (W1) who bought a Hypertronic Typewriter (W3). Enter those two model items.

(b) The relational database manager then finds the first customer in Kingston and prints her ID. It looks up on that ID to get her first transaction (W2). It also looks up the Hypertronic typewriter to get its stock number. Unfortunately the stock numbers do not match.

(c) The system searches on to get another customer in Kingston.

(d) This time the transaction Record produces a stock number that matches. Print it!

The super-form is essentially a single document. The user can move the cursor around it as one does when word processing – except, of course, that the cursor only appears inside the fields – not just anywhere on the screen. The windows holding the separate forms do not have to have borders round them: they can be merged. Thus, for instance, an invoice draws on information from the customer's name and address record, the transaction Record and the stock Record. We know that these bits come from different places in the database, but our customers neither know nor care. They want to be presented with a nice, ordinary looking invoice, and then their pens will be uncorked and they will write us a nice ordinary cheque – which was the object of the whole exercise anyway.

4.4 The problem of updating data

As so often in computing, some very nasty beasts lurk beneath the surface of database work. One of them is to do with updating Records. Our relational database has a number of Records in it which can be linked to each other by virtue of having common items. We can distinguish different Record types apart because they have other tags which are *not* in common. The user can change any item in any Record at any time. This is fine if the item being changed is a stock-holding total or a customer's address; not fine at all if it is one of the linking items. If, say, a customer's ID number got changed in the name and address Record, but not in the transactions, we would have a smashed database – there would be a customer with no business, and transactions with no person to have carried them out.

It is not good enough to assume that no one will change the ID number. Murphy's Law operates with particular virulence in computing; it is absolutely certain that such mistakes will be made and the relational database manager therefore needs some way of verifying the links set up in the database. There are many methods, of varying complexity. One, and perhaps the simplest, is just to keep a count of the number of links at each end. So, for instance, if a customer had made ten transactions, all linked to the name and address Record on his or her ID number, the system would store a link-count of ten beside it. Each of these transaction Records would be linked only once to the name and address, so they would each have a link-count of one, but there should be ten of them. The relational database manager should have some utility program that rushes round the database checking up on all the links to make sure that there are no dangling ends. If there are, they should be reported to the user for mending.

Mending the links is a relatively simple problem to solve once it is recognized as a problem at all. But there is another more insidious source of error. Suppose we have a database about customers, sales and stock (as so many are). We are recording a transaction in which a customer, written into a customer Record, comes into the shop to buy a widget. The widget is already in the database as a stock item with a supplier. The effect of the database update is to create a transaction Record with a debit to the customer and to decrease the total stock holding of widgets by one.

Here is the problem. The effect of the transaction is to alter the stock Record. Obviously it is correct in human terms to decrement the stock number by one. But as far as the database manager is concerned, this is just altering a character in a Record. Suppose, at the same time, the operator changed the source of the widget from 'Snooks and Co., Huddersfield' to 'Christian Dior, Paris'. Just more character changes to the database manager, but rather a drastic alteration from the point of view of the buying department since Christian Dior does not sell widgets.

How is the software to make sure that accidental alterations like this do not wreck the whole system? The answer is not easy. In formal terms it requires a vast apparatus of key fields, schemas, data dictionaries (Chapter 5) and the like. All this is necessary in a big mainframe database where the data is being accessed and altered by people in widely different departments who neither know nor care how the whole thing works. Probably there is no one outside the data processing department who *does* know how the whole thing works – and even inside they are not entirely sure. Happily a micro database is likely to be in more loving hands than a mainframe one. It will – or ought to – be obvious to the user that the change of supplier is not a good idea. On the other hand if the supplier has in fact changed address, it will then be a good idea to alter it in the database. With simple precautions against mistyping, and an easily intelligible database structure, one would hope that such problems can be left to the good sense of the users.

From a philosophical point of view the problem is caused by trying to make the computer mimic real objects in the real world. For the real Snooks and Co. of Huddersfield, with its furnaces and crew of taciturn Yorkshiremen, to turn itself into Dior of Paris would be a monumental undertaking. It could not possibly happen as the result of an inept keystroke. Even for the stock quantity of widgets to change, someone would have to go to the bin in the warehouse, take out a widget and lose it. Widgets, as you know, are heavy, knobbly objects made of cast iron. They do not lose easily. But the few flickers of magnetism on a disk that describe widgets lose very easily indeed.

ENQUIRY LANGUAGES

So far we have talked about fairly simple processing on the data in the database. We have assumed that when data is entered into a screen form some calculations can be done from one field to another. When it is printed out using a report generator you can also do calculations in individual Records, as well as in the Sub-total and Total lines.

However useful these facilities may be for solving many database problems they are not powerful enough to guarantee solutions to all. It is often necessary to do cleverer things and in many packages, users are given a special language to write these clever bits. These 'clever bits' are necessary to cope with problems like this: we have an employee record system which has to incorporate rules about sick-pay like these:

(1) If people are sick for less than three days, they get paid as usual unless they have used up their annual allowance of 20 sick days.

(2) If they are away sick for 3 to 40 days (not including weekends and bank holidays) the company has to make a claim on the government insurance scheme.

(3) If they are away sick more than 40 days the claim is made on the commercial pension scheme.

Or we are writing a stock control system for a clothes shop. 'Childrens' clothes, i.e. those size 10 and smaller, often bought by petite, economical ladies, do not attract 15% Value Added Tax. Our database manager has therefore got to know that:

IF SIZE < 12 THEN VAT = 0 ELSE VAT = 0.15

Or we are writing a system for an insurance company with an international sales team. If a person is a 'Regional Sales Director' he is entitled to 2.36% override on the commissions of those underneath him. A 'Continental Marketing Administrator' gets 3.96% unless he is in Arabia when he is entitled to a bag of gold of undefined size as well. To make things more interesting a person's status can change from day to day – and, moreover, in relation to other people at the same time, so that the same person may be a humble Sales Executive in North America, but in the Falkland Islands a Pan Galactic Hyper Manager entitled to an override of 6.1%. A sensible programmer will ask this particular company to take its business elsewhere, but not all perversities of real life can be dealt with in so cavalier a fashion, and there has to be some way of coping with these problems. This means a programming language of some sort.

The generic term for these languages is 'enquiry language'. Such a language has to have the essentials of all computer languages, namely:

(1) Variables able to take values – numbers, text etc. In algebra x and y stand for numbers you do not necessarily know at the time. In computing the same idea applies, but the variables generally can have more informative names like: DAILYPAYRATE or SIZE

(2) The ability to do calculations and manipulations on the variables: SPEED = DISTANCE/TIME.

(3) Test and jump facilities – IF SPEED ‹ 30 THEN PRINT 'TOO SLOW' ELSE PRINT 'WE'LL GET THERE IN GOOD TIME'. This is the crucial characteristic of a computer language. It has to be able to see if something has happened. This is done by testing a variable – in this case SPEED – to see whether it is less than 30. If it is then the program 'jumps' to the command PRINT 'TOO SLOW'. If it is not, the program looks along until it finds the word ELSE which tells it what to do in the other case – which is to print WE'LL GET THERE IN GOOD TIME.

(4) Loops – to repeat an operation several times. For instance, we want to increase the prices of all our stock items by 10%. A loop in the program is needed to find each stock Record and alter the price in it appropriately. Actually, a loop is a test and jump that goes back to the same place.

(5) These four characteristics are needed for any computer language. One that is to deal with a database also needs some means of handling the groups of variables that appear as database Records, and to do operations like joins in a relational database.

5.1 Programming languages

Most database managers provide their own enquiry languages. These are, for the most part, ordinary programming languages in function, with special commands for the special jobs that have to be done in databases. It is a matter of opinion whether the advantage of the special commands outweighs the need to learn a new language and put up with the bugs (Section 1.10) that will inevitably lurk in a newish piece of software. There is also the worry that the designers of the enquiry language did not include the very facility that – it now turns out – you need.

dBase ll, which is probably the most widely used database package for micros, has commands like:

```
                    [All ]
        DISPLAY [Record n ][OFF][FOR ‹expression›]
                    [Next n ]
```

Which, in English, is an invitation to the machine to show you records. The manual gives an example of how this construction might be used. You would write:

.DISPLAY ALL ITEM, PART:NO, COST*ON:HAND .$(PART:NO,1,2)
FOR ; COST›100 .AND. ON:HAND › 2 OFF

This produces a printout on the screen or paper like this:

TANK, SHERMAN	89793	404997.00	89
TROMBONES	76767	15076.12	76
RINGS,GOLDEN	70296	1000.00	70

The manual does not explain precisely what is going on, but presumably this is showing us the names of all stock items which cost more than £100 and of which we have more than 2, with their part numbers, cost and how many we actually have in stock.

dBASE II does have a facility for creating screen forms, which you could use to do this job in a more sympathetic way, but it is not all that easy to set up and not many people use it.

Here is an example of dBASE ll's own programming language, 'D', in which it is possible to write programs that look like*

```
        . . .
DO WHILE .NOT. EOF .AND. £ ‹= RecoCount
                &command

        IF !(Conditions) › CHR(0)
                IF &Expression
                        STORE (Count + 1) TO Count
                ENDIF
        ELSE
                STORE (Count + 1) TO Count
        ,ENDIF
        SKIP ...
```

Experience with computers suggests that the correct deployment of the many spaces, dots and exclamation marks that appear even in this small fragment of program is crucial to its operation, but it also suggests that it will be very hard to find out from the manual how to do this and even if you did there would still be surprises.

This is not very rollicking stuff. But I would not want you to think that I am particularly down on dBASE II. Here is a sample from the manual of another such product – FMS-80†

*dBASE ll Manual p 186, Ashton Tate Inc, 9929 West Jefferson Blvd., Culver City, Ca 90230.

†FMS-80 Manual p 4.2-2, DJR Associates, 2 Highland Lane, N Tarrytown, NY 10591.

```
...
/*look up the current master inventory number in the new
vendor file, and fill in the new vendor name if found
*/
                    2,2 = 1,1;                  /*inventory number*/
                    kread 2;
                    if error 2                   /*not found*/
                            3,9 = ";            /*blank name*/
                    else
                            3,9 = 2,2;
                    endif
                    write 3;
end;
...
```

The users of micro computers have been persuaded that these are, in some magical way, not programming languages, and that database packages are therefore suitable for the naive and inexperienced person. The fact is that these are programming languages much like any others and that you are not going to do well with them unless you are a reasonably experienced and determined programmer.

5.2 Programming in Superfile

When we came to consider the provision of an enquiry language for our own Superfile we came to the conclusion that a programming language is a programming language, whatever you call it; that no one who is not already a programmer is going to be able to do much with it; and that any programmer already knows at least one programming language like BASIC, PASCAL, COBOL, FORTRAN, C to name but a few. It therefore seemed pointless to inflict a *new* language, with all its inevitable faults, on him or her, so we made it possible to use any of the well proven existing languages – or even machine code – directly with Superfile.

This may have been a marketing mistake, but it certainly saved us and our customers a terrific amount of toil and trouble.

Admittedly an ordinary language will not have special database-type commands like join. But it is not hard to write subroutines which will do these things for you.

If an interpreted language like BASIC, or a program written in a compiled language, wants to use the database package directly, it has to be resident in the computer's RAM at the same time as the database package. The 16 bit operating systems have 'load and stay resident' commands which will load a program, set it running and then go off to load another program. So one would expect the database package to load and stay resident and then the program to load to use it. A memory map of the system now looks like this:

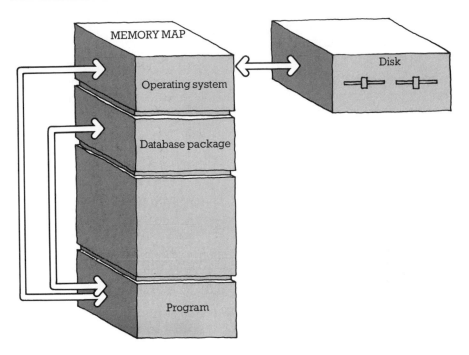

Memory map of the Superfile database manager running in a micro computer.

The program makes calls on the database package when it wants information from the database, just as it makes calls on the operating system when it wants access to files. The operating system has been enhanced by making it able to return information in useful chunks rather than just as files. Files are found by asking the operating system for them by name; data Records are found by asking for them by anything inside them, so that a Record can be thought of as a small serial file whose 'name' is anything in it.

This sort of direct access to data is rather a rarity in micro database packages, so I must fall back again on Superfile to explain how we managed the trick. A program written in BASIC uses the 'CALL' command. It has a line that looks like this in it somewhere:

CALL DBM(DF,M\$(0), R\$(0), DR)

The call command transfers program execution to the address in RAM specified by the variable DBM. This is Superfile's entry point. With it go four parameters: DF is a number that tells the database manager what to do: 11 = add a Record, 9 = find a Record, 12 = erase a Record...

The second parameter M\$(0) is a string array in which the programmer has put the text we want to send to the database. If we want to find Tom Thumb's Record, we might write this:

> M$(0) = "XNAME = Tom"
> M$(1) = "CREDIT ‹ 50"
> M$(2) = " "

That is, we are looking for a Record whose first name is 'Tom' and whose credit rating is less than 50. If we have set DF to 9, execution of the CALL command will make the database package search the database and return Tom's Record in R$:

> R$(0) = "XNAME = Tom"
> R$(1) = "XNAME = Cholmondley"
> R$(2) = "SNAME = Thumb"
> ...
> R$(n) = "CREDIT = 45"
> R$(n+1) = "CUSTID = 1543"

What one actually wants is something like Tom's credit rating. It would not be very hard to write a little BASIC subroutine which would search the Record in R$( ) to find 'CREDIT' at the left hand side of the appropriate entry and to extract the right hand side, '45'.

Doing a join with a transaction Record is hardly any more difficult. The program has to find the common tag – 'CUSTID' – extract the whole line, copy it across to R$( ) and search again from the top of the database to find Tom's transactions. If we had any more information – say that we wanted transactions where he spent more than £100, we could add it in and search with this model:

> M$(0) = "CUSTID = 1543"
> M$(1) = "PRICE › 100"
> M$(2) = " "

To do this regularly you need a subroutine called JOIN which takes as an argument the tag on which you want to link the Records – in this case CUSTID.

Programming in other languages works in much the same way.

Programming around a database really means putting the meat in a sandwich. The bottom piece of bread is the central database package which gets and stores information. The top piece of bread is the input and output from and to the real world, usually via the database manager's screen forms and reports. The meat in the middle is the program that mangles things about.

In many simple cases, where people just want to store and retrieve information, there is no filling to the sandwich – no programs are needed beyond the simple things provided in the front end. In other cases the programs produce their own outputs – data is entered through a screen form and tables are printed out directly.

The computer deals in abstractions that have to be sucked out of and returned to the real world.

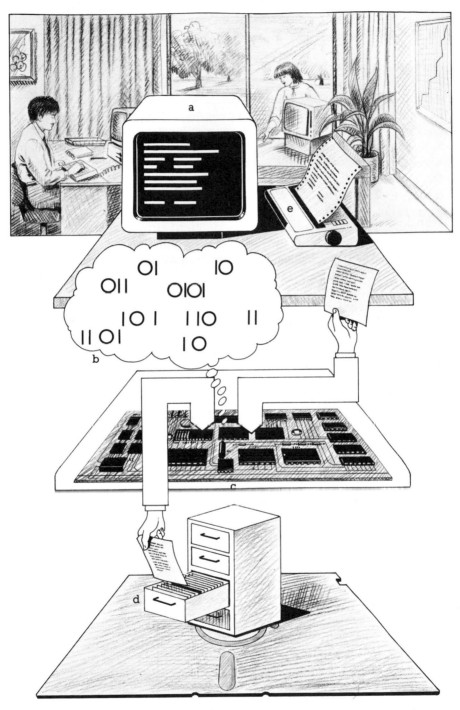

*Data is typed on the console (a), turned into bits (b)
in the processor (c), stored on disk (d),
processed and returned to the printer (e).*

5.3 A visual approach

Essentially the problem is that programming is quite different from any other human activity. To do it competently you have to have trained yourself. Learning to program is on a par with learning to drive a car with a manual gearbox, sail a boat, ride a horse or fly an aeroplane. It takes three to six months of hard work to get a start, and several years experience to become competent. Some people do it better than others and there are perfectly intelligent people who will never be able to do it at all.

However, it seems to me that programming is made harder than it need be, especially for database work. The standard programming languages are often heavily influenced by tradition and tradition in this case means a more primitive age of computing. Moreover, they are conceptually based on algebra. The programmer is expected to keep in his or her head elaborate structures of variables and pointers. The language gives very little help in manipulating the spider's web of logic that has been built up – and, predictably, programs usually end up full of bugs. Furthermore, the development of programming languages has been hampered by the tools available for programmers to work with.

Until quite recently most 'real' computing was done through punched cards or teletypes. A teletype is a crude electric typewriter: you type messages to the computer using black ink, it sends its (usually cryptic) observations back in red. This imposed a linear style on the man–machine interface which is not well suited to the way people think and in particular it does not suit the realities of database work. A database is at least a two dimensional object, and if you consider repeated fields, it has three dimensions.

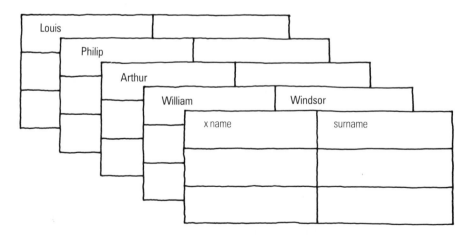

Repeated fields give rise to a three dimensional data structure.

Although I had some hard words to say about the fad for hyped-up graphics in Chapter 3, current trends in microcomputing show very clearly that people can cope much more easily with pictorial information than lines of text densely crammed with symbols. This is not surprising when you think about it, because a picture has far more data in it than the equivalent area of words. A well paid professional programmer with nothing else to think about can handle a database 'blind', using a programming language. However, the massive spread of computing means that such people are far too few on the ground to be any use. The end users must do the best they can. They will probably do it more easily if they are presented with the database in forms they can more easily understand. That means two dimensionally, visually.

The easiest way to see a Record is in the context of the form that created it – through which, in fact, the user almost certainly entered it. Any necessary explanations of what is going on can be built into the form.

Variables then are fields and their values are the contents. Suppose you had a database of modes of transport – cars, buses, bicycles, aeroplanes etc. – and in each Record, field 1 contained the name of the mode and field 5 its speed. You could rewrite the program line in (3) above (p. 100) as: IF F5 ‹ 30 THEN PRINT F1 'TOO SLOW' ELSE PRINT F1 'WILL GET US THERE IN GOOD TIME'. You would then expect to get printouts like:

BICYCLE TOO SLOW
CAR WILL GET US THERE IN GOOD TIME
DONKEY TOO SLOW
JET PLANE WILL GET US THERE IN GOOD TIME

...

Databasish things like joins can also be done visually. We saw in Chapter 4 how a screen forms generator based on windowed word processing can display several different forms – and their Records – in different windows on the screen, and can automatically link the Records in a relational way by copying the contents of the shared field from one form to the other. That gives us visual analogies for two of the three things an enquiry language ought to do: allow the use of variables and calculations on them. The last, providing tests and jumps, does not seem to have any visual analogy. You have to write these in a program-like way. But at least the IF's and ELSEs can refer to visible fields. This stage can be handled by putting up the form(s) on the screen, going through the fields one by one and asking their creator to enter any formulae to go with each field. For instance: we are trying to cope with the sick employees problem:

Here we have two simple Records: an employee's name and address and one of his sickness absences. They are linked by his unique employee number field. The automatic relational features of the forms package mean that we can consider each presentation of a linked pair of such Records as a

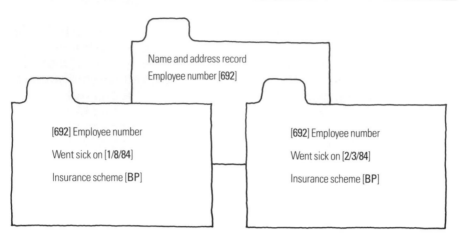

An employee Record and two related sick Records.

single virtual Record so that if we need to we can include values from any of the fields in either of the forms in our calculations of formulae.

Each field is identified by a pair of letters running from 'aa' to 'ad' (since in this case there are four fields shown). The system has put a star in the 'ad' field, which means that it is asking us to define a formula for it. The effect we are trying to achieve is to separate our sick employees into three classes: those who have been sick less than 3 days (class A); those who have been sick between 3 and 40 days (class B) and, the more than 40s (class C). We might write:

**IF TODAYDATE – AC ‹ 3 THEN AD = 'A' OR IF TODAYDATE – AC › 3
AND TODAYDATE – AC ‹= 40 THEN AD = B ELSE AD = C'.**

('TODAYDATE' is a variable holding today's date that gets filled in from the computer's internal calendar clock.) Another form or a bit of program deals with the three classes and what is to be done about them.

Of course this is all a bit simple-minded because the real sick pay legislation talks about 'working days' so we have to ignore Saturdays and Sundays. One can cope with that reasonably easily by dividing the Julian day number by 7 and looking at the remainder. A remainder of 6, for instance, might mean the day is a Tuesday. But it is all more complicated again than that because we have to take into account public holidays – which are, by definition, not 'working days'. Probably we shall have to create a third form that just deals with this problem by looking at the dates of holidays in the database. (I mention all this just to show that programming is not easy, whatever name it goes by.)

5.4 Schemas and data dictionaries

A couple of words and phrases from big computing occasionally crop up in micro database work: 'schema' and 'data dictionary'. It may be worth having an idea what they mean, even though few micro implementations of database managers will use them explicitly.

A data dictionary is 'data about data' (Date, 1981). It contains descriptions of all the major objects in the system – the types of item and record, who uses them and with what programs. The point of the data dictionary is to help the human Database Administrator – known as the 'DBA' in the trade – to maintain the database. If the DBA wants to enlarge the scope of a particular Record, he or she can see from the dictionary what programs have to be changed and what human users have to be warned that their screens are going to look different.

The 'conceptual schema' is the ideal definition of the data. It describes what is to be stored in a form which makes no reference to a particular computer installation. It is concerned with the shapes of Records, data types, access codes and the like. It is part of the data dictionary. The 'internal schema' is wholly concerned with the computer. It is concerned with how this particular machine is to implement the conceptual schema. It is to do with field lengths, indexing, hashing, pointers – in fact most of the things that are provided automatically by a micro database manager and are often kept invisible from the user.

5.5 PROLOG

A perennial source of amusement to computer people is the debate about languages. Is BASIC better than PASCAL? Is COBOL better than death? That sort of thing, and rather a waste of time too. A slightly more interesting implementation of the argument is about the alternative merits of 'von Neumann' and 'list processing' languages. A von Neumann language, named after the elegant refugee from Hitler's Germany who signally helped the US get into computing during World War II, is like BASIC, PASCAL, FORTRAN, C. It is essentially an authoritarian list of commands that the computer is to execute. Smart ones allow the programmer to write 'procedures', self contained tools that can be used by other procedures, and very smart ones are 'recursive', which means that a procedure can call itself.

Implicit in the von Neumann view of programming is that the programmer knows what he or she wants to do in detail. He or she builds the detail up into a program and when finished stops.

A list processing language works quite differently. There you start with some grand overall statement† like:

MEANING UNIVERSE(GODS,MEN)

You then try to flesh out this good beginning with some subsidiary statements like:

NATURE(MEN,MORTAL)
NATURE(GODS,IMMORTAL)

You keep going until you get down to things that the computer can cope with on its own like $2 + 2 = 4$. At that point you stop. If all the links if the chain are sound you have a program which, in this case, will perhaps tell you the meaning of the universe.

The point of this diversion is to introduce PROLOG, a list processing language that is now much in favour among the artificial intelligence community. The Japanese like it because (so it is said) some stupid or unscrupulous person told them that PROLOG was formalized English and that if they could understand PROLOG they could understand the Western language as well.

PROLOG expects to be fed with relationships like:

likes(joe,fish)
likes(joe,mary)
likes(mary,book)
likes(john,book)

You can then ask it questions (the computer's answers are in bold)

?- likes(joe,money)
no
?- likes(mary,book)
yes

and so on. This is trivial stuff and it only becomes useful and interesting when the likes and dislikes are much more complicated; when you can ask things like: ' Find me someone who likes someone who likes books and fish and doesn't like someone who dislikes fish but likes football.'

The point that interests us here is that PROLOG is essentially a very powerful relational database enquiry language, but one, in most implementations, without a database manager. It expects to keep all its information in RAM, which means that its database can be no bigger than tiny and rather limits the usefulness of the thing. An interface between PROLOG and good information management system might be a useful beast.

†I will take the liberty of quoting from myself, since I can't think of a better way to explain the matter. See Laurie (1983).

You could then have a database system that held people and projects in, say, the film industry. You might be able to explore the film-makers' world of contacts and personal associations by asking questions like: 'Find me people who have worked on at least two films with anyone who has worked on a film that grossed more than £50 million and has never worked on a film that has lost money.' That way you might get a rather competent crew together. You might also impose guilt by association, a doctrine that the courts take great care to outlaw.

CHAPTER SIX

DATA: SOURCES AND COSTS

Until recently, most work on microcomputers was done with word processing or spread sheet packages. They produced reasonably small files and if they, or the machine, or the operator, blundered, no great harm was done. It is annoying to lose a chapter of a book or a cash flow, but not disastrous. Database work is rather different. The data may well be more expensive to acquire than the cost of the software and the hardware on which it runs. But the cost of losing it may be much more yet: it could well put the enterprise out of business.

How much does data cost? This is not a very important question now except to data publishers, but it will become more and more important to everyone who uses micros in the future. There are several components. Firstly the data has to be acquired. It has to appear in some form on paper on someone's desk ready to be typed in. It could be the results of a house to house survey, a government census, the response to an advertising campaign. It can hardly cost less than 10p a Record to get it there and the cost may well be many times this, so let us put in 50p as a maximum and 25p as a sensible average. It then has to be typed in: a good typist can do about 50 words a minute when it is bitty work like this. Allow 6 bytes to the word, so that is 300 bytes a minute and 300B makes a reasonable database Record.

A typist costs, with overheads, at least £10 000 a year or about 10p a minute. Allow the same cost again for verification of the data (see below for a discussion of necessity of verification), and then a charge for the capital and maintenance costs of the machine on which the data is held. If we allow a minimum of £4000 to buy a machine suitable for serious database work, with hard disk (say 15MB) and printer, the interest, capital repayment over five years and annual maintenance charges will total about £1800 a year. The smallest database that is worth keeping would have about 3000 300B Records – it would be about 1MB in size. The cost per Record for acquisition would be 45p or £1350. Each year one can expect roughly 20% (this may be more or less, depending on the application) of the Records to change, so maintenance will cost another £270 per year.

Even a small database like this costs £3150 in the first year and £2070 thereafter – and this ignores the salary and overheads of the executive who supervises the project. If we costed in his or her grey hairs it might be twice as expensive.

People are beginning to think about much bigger databases on micros. For instance, some British Members of Parliament want to keep databases on all their constituents. Come election time, they want to be able to send well-tailored mail shots to the blue collar workers, and different shots to the white collars. The MPs want to be able to write personally to all the people who are members of conservation organizations to boast about their wonderful voting record on seal culling and deforestation. And, conversely, they want to be able to send letters to all the voters who would rather be dead than red, pointing out their representative's wonderfully hard record on all questions of foreign and military policy.

However attractive such an exercise might be in theory, it can turn out to be very expensive in practice. An average constituency has about 60 000 voters. Their names and addresses are available from the Town Hall on paper (the Home Office has them all on computer tape, but refuses to release them because of paranoia about Data Protection – see Section 6.4) so they have to be typed in by hand.

A 60 000 Record database (again, assuming 300B per Record) will take up 18MB of space and its indexes will need at least another 18MB. This means a fairly substantial micro, if only because entering and maintaining a database of this size will need the efforts of several people and the hardware will therefore have to be multi-user. Put in £16 000 for machinery: the annual hardware cost (calculated in the same way as before) will be £7200. The cost of the data might be something like £27 000 to begin with (the voter's list is free, but there will usually be an acquisition cost for the data in most other applications) and £5400 a year for data maintenance. The whole proposition begins to look quite expensive. Even if it is worth the cost, it is important to bear in mind that any useful parcel of data can easily cost more than the software and the hardware combined. It is therefore very foolish to try to save money on cheap hardware or software which might put the integrity of your data at risk.

If you can, it would make more sense to buy the data than type it in. Of course there are many databases that cannot ever be bought – a firm's customers or employees and the state of their accounts cannot be got from anyone else. But a database of potential widget buyers for a firm that makes widgets can certainly be bought. It will be got from specialists who do nothing but collect this sort of information. They will hold databases on everything that every company in an industry or geographical area buys and can then extract from it those that are of interest to the widget maker. This sort of thing has been going on, in a crude way, for years in the form of mailing lists. You can, if you want, buy lists of addresses of people and businesses who are interested in the most obscure things. You want teachers who book holiday travel? You want diving companies who buy hydrogen gas? Somebody, somewhere, has a little list.

In the past you bought the list just as names and addresses on computer tape or printed out onto gum-on mailing labels. You would use the list to mail out your brochures and hope that you got enough leads back to make the whole operation worthwhile. It could all be much better if you could build up your own database. You might start by buying, on floppy disk, a list of widget users. You put the list into your own database on your own micro, which now holds in it all your potential customers. You mail them all, using your database manager's facility for printing mailing labels and then you enter the responses you have had. This company has moved. That company would like your sales representative to call. This third company actually now buy more wodgets than widgets and can you help? Soon you have added so much more useful information that the data you bought in the first place is hardly recognizable.

As soon as your sales drive starts to work the list of propects begins to turn into a list of customers. You begin to add transaction records and to acquire material for your book-keeping programs that also look at the database.

Until recently, we have assumed that all the data in a micro is created by its users. If you concede that a software package running on a micro is a bit like following the instructions in a 'how to' book, the present age of computing is a bit like the first days of printing, when the difficult bit was actually making marks on paper. To go back to the useful analogy of Caxton: when he set up shop, people hardly worried about writing manuscripts for publication. There were no professional writers, no agents, no editors or publishers. Anything reasonably readable could be set in print and would find a customer or two. Four hundred years later, the emphasis in book publishing is on writing. It is much easier to print something than to find something worthwhile to print. We will, no doubt, see the same change in computing. At the moment we give people a microcomputer and say, in effect, 'Using this you can write your own dictionary, telephone directory, tax guide and hundreds of other useful books. Have a nice day.' Some of us could physically write these books if we tried hard enough and had nothing else to do, but it is much easier to let someone else do the work. It is much cheaper too, because they can spread the costs over a large number of customers. The same thing applies to software and data.

6.1 Distributing data

If we make the (quite reasonable) analogy between filled databases and books, the obvious question arises of distribution. A book is no commercial good – i.e. it won't get published – unless it can be put in as many customers' hands as possible and as much money as possible got back from them. In parallel with the 400 years of advance in printing technology has gone an equal advance in marketing. We now have well-organized markets and channels of distribution for printed information products.

The most important thing is that there are large numbers of discriminating customers in the English speaking world who know how a book ought to look, feel, weigh, cost. They are crucial to a well-formed market.

Why, one might ask, does a person generally eat better in France than in America or Britain? The two latter countries probably have better raw materials and certainly France has no monopoly on intelligent chefs. The crucial difference is that French restaurant customers would, sooner than put up with the garbage generally eaten in Anglo-Saxon countries, make their way to the kitchen and spit the first mouthful into the cook's face. It does wonders for cooks, that kind of thing. In the same way the book market knows what a bookshop ought to be like and roughly where to find it. The shops are served by distributors who can supply the books that the customers want. The distributors are served by publishers who have money to invest in new books and who know what sorts of books are worth what effort. They can find people to produce, edit, proof-read these books and finally, working backwards, there are large numbers of literate people who have acquired information which is worth putting into books to serve as authors.

Well, hardly anything like this is available in the microcomputer market, and the database market has hardly begun. There is a fair amount of data available on big computers, but the channels of distribution are pretty crude. There are about 1500 databases world-wide maintained on mainframes and sold to specialist users. For example: Reuters stock market figures, the Lexis legal database, Datasolve's World Reporter international news service. To access these you need a telephone line, a micro, a modem (see Section 1.8) and a lot of patience because they all work differently.

But the most serious drawback is that they are electronic imitations of paper systems. You put in a request for information, the computer sorts through it and sends back the data you want. It appears on your computer screen, you read it and that is that. You cannot easily build the information directly into your own database. You cannot easily pull down a subset of the main database to build on it. You cannot sell your data back to improve the main one.

The obvious way to improve on this is to sell pre-filled databases on disk to run under existing database management software – providing, of course, that the software will allow the expansion of Records. Users can then add their own data to what they buy and, in principle, sell it back to the data publisher. There should eventually be a two-way traffic. One factor that has held this up so far in the history of microcomputing is the absence of a standard disk format. Admittedly, 8″ IBM single sided, single density disks are the same on all machines that have them, but very few do. Unhappily most micro manufacturers chose 5¼″ disks and then went on to invent their own disk standards. There are now some 200 different ways of writing a 5¼″ disk. This imposes a nightmare on software publishers and has made data publishing – where updates may need to be weekly – quite out of the question. The database business also needed the widespread use of hard disks to make it possible for users to keep reasonably comprehensive databases. Both of these problems are beginning to be solved by the emergence of the IBM Personal Computer as a practical standard. Most 16 bit machines running under MS-DOS or CP/M 86 will now read PC format disks, and 'industry observers' (those vague people who always say what the person quoting them thinks) opine that by 1986 there will be some 9 million business micros in the US and 1 million in the UK. That begins to make quite a sizeable marketplace. Many machines of this type (including, of course, the IBM XT) have hard disks and the cost of this hardware is falling all the time. The conditions are now ripe for a micro information industry. Although much reviled by advocates of the 'wired society', in which everyone has enormously high capacity fibre optic data paths to their homes and offices, a computer disk through the post is a very quick and convenient way of exchanging data. Let us just look at the immediate alternative: data down the phone line. The fastest practicable data rate is

1500 bits per second over ordinary domestic lines. The normal rate, and the fastest if one assumes that one end is using a cheap audio coupled modem, is 300 bits per second. A useful commercial database might run to 5MB and would take no less than 37 hours to transmit at 300 bits/s. It would be most surprising if the data came across clean at the first attempt, so the actual transmission time might run to a week or more. The postman looks positively dynamic by comparison.

However it might be possible to find a compromise between the complete personal database on a desk-top micro in the user's office and the impersonal mainframe database that just delivers one-off responses. What is happening and will doubtless develop in many ways we cannot yet foresee is the electronic mailbox business. A mailbox system is a database held on a large computer with access to the telephone network. One example is the *British Telecom Gold* which connects directly to ITT's *Dialcom* in the USA, and to similar systems in 18 or more other countries. Each customer has a mailbox with a number, e.g. '81:ABC123'. The first two digits say that the customer is on computer 81 – one of the two that serve London. The three letters identify him or her and the three digits identify one of the many possible mailboxes used. To use the system you either ring

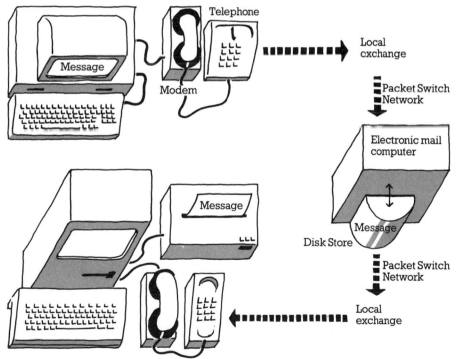

In an electronic mail system, subscribers use their computers to send and receive messages from a database on a big computer.

the computer's telephone number direct, or if you live more than a local call away you dial into the Packet Switched Network and get cheap access that way. Many micros now have built in modems and automatic dialling equipment. Suitable software will ring the system and log on automatically.

Each customer's mailbox is in effect a Record in a database. The database is spread over many different computers, but the system handles the interconnections automatically. Subscribers can write messages to each other's mailboxes and so carry on a sort of telex-like conversation – but much more easily and naturally. If a group of subscribers have a common mailbox they can have 'meetings' with each other by writing notes on a subject of common interest. You log on, read your mail, look at the latest contribution to the subject under discussion, go back check old Bill's observations and write your own little bit pointing out the fallacy of Allan's idea but drawing attention to something Jean said three weeks ago which now becomes relevant. People working for the same department of a company can be linked by mailbox as intimately as if they were in the same office even though they are thousands of miles apart.

The beauty of a mailbox system on a central computer is that they do not stop at the user's VDU. It can just as well be a personal computer that sends enquiries to the system, and those enquiries can be passed by the mailbox database to another computer with a database. A mailbox system obviously provides an excellent method for distributing data. A user of a database sends an enquiry – 'Please give me all the potential widget buyers in Manitoba who employ more than 50 people.' The mailbox system passes it on to the appropriate database (there will be databases of databases), pays for the information, debits the enquirer's account and puts the results in her mailbox. She can then download it into her own database and get on with the job. In time she will acquire just the data she needs, when she needs it.

6.2 Computerizing all sorts of data

It is rather difficult to predict just what form pre-filled databases might take. One might imagine that the normal reference books one sees in any office will go straight across – telephone books, trade directories, catalogues, dictionaries – anything in lists has an obvious counterpart in databases. But it is also possible that the whole trend of database development – although dealing in the same information as on paper – may organize it quite differently.

The most obvious source, the telephone book, is an interesting example. In it one has, essentially, a register of all the economically and socially active people in a community. One has their names, telephone numbers, addresses and post codes. This is all fine, but there is other very useful information that could be added. Whenever we meet someone new we want to know 'what they do' and roughly what they earn. (In American you can just ask their earnings; in Britain you have to go through tremendous social contortions to find out.) Well, this information is available – sort of – in the returns from the five-yearly Census. The Census authorities have access to the individual returns; in the UK, to preserve people's confidentiality, you can only get data at the 100-household level. But people of a kind tend to live together, so that could be quite useful.

Unfortunately this is a very big database. The UK census uses some 100 000 Records, each with about 4000 three digit fields to describe the population.

2 All residents

Age	TOTAL PERSONS	Males		Females		Ret'd Males
		SWD	Mrr'd	SWD	Mrr'd	
TOTAL	50	52	53	55	56	190
0-4	57	59	xxx	62	xxx	xxx
5-9	64	66	xxx	69	xxx	xxx
10-14	71	73	xxx	76	xxx	xxx
15	78	80	xxx	83	xxx	xxx
16-19	85	87	88	90	91	xxx
20-24	92	94	95	97	98	xxx
25-29	99	101	102	104	105	xxx
30-34	106	108	109	111	112	xxx
35-39	113	115	116	118	119	199
40-44	120	122	123	125	126	200
45-49	127	129	130	132	133	201
50-54	134	136	137	139	140	202
55-59	141	143	144	146	147	203
60-64	148	150	151	153	154	204
65-69	155	157	158	160	161	205
70-74	162	164	165	167	168	206
75-79	169	171	172	174	175	207
80-84	176	178	179	181	182	208
85+	183	185	186	188	189	209

5 All residents aged 16 or over

Economic Position	TOTAL PERS	Males		Females	
		SWD	Mrr'd	SWD	Mrr'd
ALL PERSONS 16+	380	382	383	385	386
Total econ active	387	389	390	392	393
Working	394	396	397	399	400
Seeking work	401	403	404	406	407
Temp sick	408	410	411	413	414
Total econ inact	415	417	418	420	421
Perm sick	422	424	425	427	428
Retired	429	431	432	434	435
Student	436	438	439	441	442
Other inactive	443	445	446	448	449

Extract from one of the many pages of the UK Census giving data on a specific area.

This is 1.2GB (a gigabyte = 1 000 000 000 bytes) and not really a practical proposition until next year's laser disks are on the market (see Section 1.9). However, you can get the same data aggregated into about 10 000 local voting wards, which each contain roughly 5000 people or 1000 households. Many people in marketing and distribution would dearly like to have this sort of data on their desk-top micros. As an executive in one of Britain's largest companies told me: 'If you cost distribution properly, including capital tied up in inventory, management, warehousing, movement of goods, it comes to some 40% of all your costs. You don't have to make much of an improvement there to have a whole bundle of money in your hand. The essential tool is this sort of database.'

One can see that the Census database could be vastly improved. One would want to know not only about the people in a ward – how much they earn, how many bedrooms in their houses, how many cars they drive, but also about the businesses there. How many major grocery outlets, garages, factories and what do they make? What commercial TV area is it in? What post codes attach to the streets in it?

Our friend the widget maker started a database from a list of potential widget customers. There is no reason why this should not be part of a much grander, all-embracing database of everyone, every enterprise, everybody's qualifications and interests both professional and private. It would have every person's location in the social sense – where they live, what job they do and where they do it, and if relevant, where they are at that particular moment of time. If they were interested in another job the database might store that information so that potential employers could get in touch. It would have mailboxes so that you could send messages. It would identify club memberships so that something of interest to stamp collectors could be sent to them all automatically. If you have things to sell the database will convey the information automatically to people who want to buy. The system might also act as a bank so that you put money into it and you can use credits to trade electronically.

So much of this information could only be supplied by the person involved that involvement in the system would have to be voluntary. If by the year 2000 you want to live a full social and professional life your entry in the 'telephone book' will have to be very full and very up to date. If you want to retire from the world you just erase yourself. If you are fed up with stamp collectors you put a security code on that entry so that only your friends who have the code can see it. Security will obviously be most important. There are things you want your friends to know that you do not want broadcast to the world. The database managers that run these systems will have to have hierarchies of very elaborate security checks. They will also have to validate certain items of information so that someone who claims to be a doctor will be guaranteed by the database to be one. We will have to have electronic equivalents to the signature on paper to authenticate documents and transactions.

There is no limit either to the level of detail that might be available. At the moment we have to deal with things in the millions by very rough statistical processes. Our governments are elected for five year terms by what a majority thought about some vague promises on a certain day. When these real-time on-line databases are working it will be possible to have instant votes on any number of subjects. Your vote on any contemporary issue is just an item in your personal Record. This might be possible, but possibly not desirable because what an electorate votes for is not so much a package of policies as a person who looks as if he or she might behave sensibly in the unknown emergencies that will face a government. The voter will not have studied the issues and is possibly not mentally capable of making much sense of them. Instant electronic democracy might prove to be a complete curse – like letting the passengers on a bus have a steering wheel each and using a computer to work out an average of them all to steer the actual vehicle.

We do not have to be as advanced as that to get some very interesting effects. At the moment, in the distribution of resources, we are as general as in politics. If you want to fly the Atlantic you first have to choose an airline, then you see if they have a flight at the right time and then whether there is a free seat. What you as a passenger actually want is a seat going to New York at the right time and price. In most cases it is unimportant what airline offers it – they are all equally revolting. A publicly available database of flights that started with unsold seats and worked backwards to airlines would be much more useful. If it were combined with a ticketing system so that the occupied seats represented definite travellers the whole nightmare of flight booking would disappear – and it would save the airlines a tremendous number of staff because the customers with their own computers would do all the work.

All sorts of goods could be sold in the same way. Houses, cars – even packets of washing powder. If and when high resolution datalinks are available to most people's homes and offices, we can have high quality pictures along with text.

6.3 Accuracy

So far we have talked as if all the data in a database were automatically true, accurate and above-board. This is not necessarily so. An essential, though little appreciated function of the book publisher is sub-editing. The sub-editor tries to take care that each book is accurate, literately expressed, and conforms to the often unconscious norms that people apply to that sort of book. For instance you would not expect footnotes in a light romance, or a paragraph in a directory to the world jute market that began: 'It was a dark and stormy night...'.

It is the editor's job to supervise what goes into the book on behalf of the publisher and the resultant guarantee of quality is encapsulated in the 'imprint', the publisher's trade mark. One good reason why people take trouble to get books right is that they are very expensive to make. The cheapest book costs its publisher some 10 to 20 thousand pounds. Most of this money goes on paper, printing and physical distribution, and is, of course, saved in electronic publishing. Instead the consumer buys a computer and pays for the telephone line. In principle this is excellent, since it favours the small, independent customer over the commercial monolith. In practice it is not all unalloyed joy because the costs of verification, which can easily be as much as capturing the data in the first place, now become a very large part of the cost of the whole database, rather than a small proportion as in the paper version. The temptation will be to skimp the expensive process of verification – just as small airlines tend to skimp the necessary but unglamorous business of maintaining their aircraft. As the careless shipwright said of the hole in the bottom of the boat – 'They'll never see it – it'll be underwater.'

The trouble with mistakes in data or books is that they are invisible until they bite you – unless you take the trouble to look for them first. I wish I had £5 for every time a programmer has said to me: 'There are no more bugs in this piece of software.', only to come back a week (or worse, 6 months) later with 'I can't see how it could ever have worked!' The same thing applies to data. It is going to cost data publishers a lot more than they think to get data right, and until they can guarantee accuracy people are going to have to be rather suspicious. Imagine, for instance, the performance of a piece of software that automatically managed your stock exchange investments if the price data it started with was wrong.

Inaccuracy will become a big problem with electronic publishing – and it is already appearing in some American university campuses where everyone is fashionably 'on line'. Much of the course work consists of text written by the staff and distributed by computer. Not suprisingly it contains mistakes, blunders, short cuts. If it had gone through even the modest publishing process of copy-editing necessary in the pre-computer age, many of these shortcomings would have appeared. Similar criticisms have been levelled at packages for teaching mathematics in the UK.

One of the attractions of computer data is that it always *looks* right. One of the more useful software tools on most people's micros is a spread sheet calculator. I often use mine to prepare cash flow reports about our business. Recently I did one that showed unusually encouraging figures. Our bank manager was thrilled with it and took it hotfoot to some chums in a venture capital outfit. They loved it. Everyone was most happy until I discovered that the good effect was due to the spread sheet only adding up half of each monthly column of costs. The error was apparent on the paper to anyone who studied the figures with the least attention because they looked like this:

Wages	6000
Rent	2000
Ads	26000
Telephone	500
Total	8000

but of course, nobody did, because it looked so *right*.

The formula for getting the total had added only the first two rows. The formula had accidentally got changed at some earlier stage in the spread sheet's history and no one had noticed – because, of course, the whole purpose of the computer was to save the brain-ache of actually adding up the figures. So no one did.

One must assume that *everything* in a computer is wrong until proved otherwise. And the only convincing proof is long usage. If a piece of data or of software has been in constant use for many years by many people without complaint then one can assume that it works reasonably well. Of course the whole assumption about on-line databases is that the information in them is always new – and therefore, almost by definition, inaccurate.

6.4 Data protection laws

Another coming complication to the widespread use of databases is forthcoming data protection legislation in the UK. In principle the purpose of these laws is:

(1) To enable people to be sure that data about them held on computer is accurate.
(2) That if it is confidential – for instance, medical records – only those people who ought to be able to see it, can.

The proposal is that people who want to keep databases will have to be licenced and that anyone who feels that the data about them in a database is wrong should be able to see it and challenge the inaccuracies. Apart from wondering why this idea should only apply to computer databases when for a long time those kept on paper have been much bigger and potentially more harmful, it is very hard to see how it can possibly work when each one of millions of personal computers may hold a database. By 1990, printout listing the possible databases in which one's name might be mentioned might well weigh half a ton. It would take a lifetime just to read through it.

The second requirement of the data protection Act is either easier or harder to satisfy. It either merely demands modest security features which can quite easily be implemented; or completely uncrackable codes which cannot.

6.5 The obsolescence of history

Another worrying feature of electronic publishing is its immediacy. A piece of information changes and everyone concerned has their copy of the database updated immediately. The old version has gone for ever. A great virtue of print was that everything was produced in vast numbers. Once a piece of type had been set up, economics made it sensible to print as many copies as possible because they were so cheap. The result was and is that hardly anything that has been set in print gets lost. Many libraries round the world file daily newspapers. Every copy of every book is sent to at least one national library for safekeeping, and in most cases to many. Quite apart from this formal archiving, anything that is produced in thousand or hundreds of thousands must leave some survivors to posterity. Copies lodge in bottom drawers, in out of the way libraries, in attics and trunks and are found again, perhaps many centuries later.

To many orthodox organizations like the Catholic Church the invention of printing was a mixed blessing. While it allowed the faithful to spread the word more cheaply than before, it also allowed the heretical to spread their (wrong) version of the word just as easily. Over the centuries many books have been published that the Vatican would have liked to see disappear. Yet it has succeeded, in only a very few cases, in handing a complete edition to the hangman for burning, and most of those were published in a language like Tuscan which gave them no readership outside the physical area controlled by the Roman Catholic Church. A heretical book in Latin or even Italian would find readers all over Europe, would fly hither and yon and instantly be beyond the reach of the hangman. Historians of printing and publishing have found at least one copy of pretty well every book that is known to have been printed in the Western world in the last five hundred years.

Even State secrets had to be written down and kept somewhere – often in several different places by different people. As a result there are few unsolved political mysteries in the last five hundred years of European history. It would be well if one could hope the same of the next five hundred years. The speed and evanescence of electronic data means that there is only one copy at a time of any information – the new, up-to-date, correct one. Archiving will not happen in the way of nature, it will have to be done consciously. And whatever is done consciously is always done badly.

Libraries are very expensive things to collect, to house and to maintain. But until now there has been no alternative. Any seat of learning – even one as humble as a primary school – has to have a library. A university has something valued in billions of pounds. But come electronics, people will get out of the way of keeping libraries – they will become expensive luxuries. There will be nowhere to store even those scraps of paper that do survive the electronic blizzard. History will vanish. It was been rightly said that a people that has no history has no future. History is the great corrector of all sorts of personal and social folly. It teaches that the world has its own great rules which are ignored at one's peril. The first action of the tyrant is always to rewrite history in some way or another. The great defence of the people is to be able to find out what really happened. Just because electronics is modern we need not think that it will make tyrants old-fashioned. And there is nothing a tyrant likes better than to find no record of the past to contradict what he says happened.

CHAPTER SEVEN

THE INTELLIGENT DATABASE

The phrase 'artificial intelligence' (usually abbreviated to 'AI'), must have struck anyone who is even vaguely interested in computing. AI has grown up into a world of its own that promises, so its devotees insist, wonderful things. There is also a school of thought that holds that AI is as empty and fraudulent as phrenology. Still, if taken not too seriously, AI has some interesting implications for database work.

The essential distinction between ordinary programming and AI is that in the former, programmers are assumed to know what they want the computer to do in the minutest detail. The difficulty is to make it do it. In AI the programmers do *not* know what they want the computer to do. Instead they have an idea how they could make the computer find out what is to be done. They write a program to do this and watch the results with interest. There is a saying in the trade: 'If you understand how it works, it isn't AI.' There is a shorter, cynical version too: 'If it works, it isn't AI.'

How would AI be applied to a database manager? How would an 'intelligent' database work?

It is estimated that when a doctor makes a diagnosis he has to take into account nearly a million separate items of information. 'Expert systems' running on micros are beginning to help with this task.

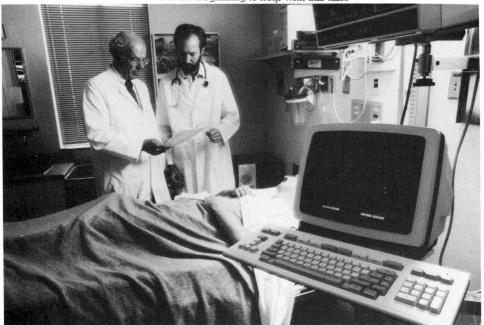

So far, the best known product of AI is the 'expert system' – an intelligent database would be its inverse. But first to explain how an expert system works. It is a program which allows a human expert who has, either by personal research and experience or by proxy through an educative process managed by other people, digested large numbers of facts, to extract rules from them. The expert system then organizes the rules so that they can be stored in the computer and consulted by non-expert human users.

For instance, an expert system about managing disasters on oil rigs would hold information gathered from people who understand oil wells and their troubles. These people would, one hopes, have considered all the permutations of unpleasantness that could befall an oil rig manager. They would have asked themselves what he should do if the fuel tanks for the helicopter go on fire. What action should he take if the well-head valves fail? What is to be done if one of the rig's legs buckles? All these problems interact on each other in a complicated way which the manager may not have time to unravel in the heat of the moment. Given a computer and an expert system, the beleaguered rig manager should be able to tell it his troubles and get constructive advice back.

From one point of view an expert system just creates a 'soft' index to a body of knowledge. If you had a handbook of rig disasters you could look through the index for the signs of the particular disaster that threatened you:

...

Fires	p. 45
Fires, helicopter fuel	p. 57
Fires with ship impact	p. 84

...

An expert system will do better than that. Like a database, it will allow you to search on several things at once: fire, fuel, shipwreck. It will also ask how sure you are that the indications you are searching with are true. As a rig manager awoken from a dreamless sleep by a red glare at your porthole, you might not be sure what was on fire. If asked by the system how sure you were that the fuel tanks for the rig's helicopter were burning, you might have to answer '50%' – or 'not very'.

Such systems are used seriously in, for instance, the diagnosis of disease. 'How sure are you that the patient has drunk contaminated water in the last month?' The doctor may not know and the patient may be too sick to tell her, so she has to guess. The system may ask her to guess on a scale of 1 (definitely no) to 5 (definitely yes) and she enters 4 – 'maybe', because she knows that the poor patient has just come back from a difficult trans-Sahara expedition. And so the system goes on, asking sensible questions. When it has the data, it can make an estimate of the disease: 'Bilharzia 80%, Malaria 45%'.

It is important to bear in mind that today's 'expert systems' encapsulate the knowledge of human experts. They do *not* let the computer find out anything for itself. That would be done by an 'intelligent database'. It would do the reverse of such a trick. It would run around a database full of facts – histories of accidents on oil rigs and what was done about them – and extract from the data a set of rules. These rules would be expressed either as statements in a human-like language which would convey the substance of them to a person so that he or she can make the appropriate decisions on new data; or as programs which will allow the computer to make the same decisions automatically.

For example, in a commercial setting we might expect the intelligent database containing a firm's trading records to examine customers and try to deduce the characteristics of potential debtors. In a medical setting we might expect to deduce the outcome of heart attacks or the causes of fevers.

In many cases the database will have been collected for ordinary data processing purposes. The deduction of rules from it will be an incidental benefit as far as the user is concerned. If the rule(s) turn out to be useful and reliable the side-effect will have been profitable; otherwise it will have been a waste of time.

Alternatively, the data will have been collected as part of a research project. For example a scientist might be investigating the incidence of leprosy in villages in Africa. She collects a database of the condition of life in villages where people got leprosy: how many people shared the water, how many dogs in the village, what sanitation, what plants grow around the village etc. It is possible that when the data is in, the rule that predicts leprosy is evident on inspection. Leprosy and stray dogs go together. It is more likely that the rule (if there is one) may be quite invisible to the naked eye. A rule finder might be the only way to discover what is hidden in the data. And the rule could be quite esoteric. It might turn out that leprosy goes with villages where many plants grow whose names begin with the letter 'b'. And why? Because in the M'bongo language (as spoken locally) purple things have names beginning with 'b'. The plants that grow in leprosy villages are purple because the soil there contains large amounts of antimony. The rule finder seems to have discovered a new medical fact – that leprosy and antimony in the soil go together.

This example supposes a rather sophisticated system: one that could do string analysis on the names of objects to find out that they began with 'b' and is not very practical in the current state of software development.

How might one build a practical intelligent database? At the moment we do not really know what will work best and we must experiment with a range of theoretical approaches to see which meshes best with the data real users produce and the skills they can bring to bear on it. There are a number of options open to us, ranging from classical statistical analysis,

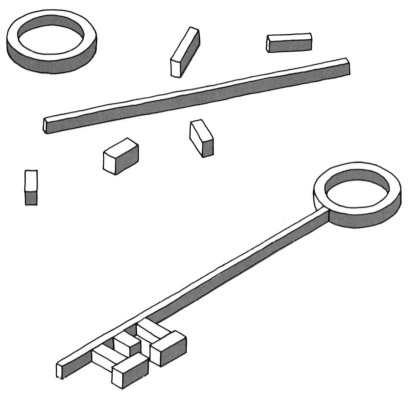

The inverse of expert system that applies human rules to data, is the rule finder that searches for regularities in what otherwise seems unrelated data.

through Bayesian logic which deals not just with Yes and No, True and False, but with probabilities, to random rule generation with natural selection.

A good starting point is a package called *Analogue Concept Learning System** – also marketed as *Expertease* – written by people at the Machine Intelligence Unit, Edinburgh University under the direction of Professor Donald Michie.

The original function of ACLS was to look at tables of facts entered specially into the program and, using Bayesian logic, to deduce from them rules connecting single variables. For instance, you might have tables of tests to be applied to finished parts in an engineering shop. Each part must weigh between this and that, be so long plus or minus so much, be that wide etc. These tables can often run to thousands of items: ACLS can often boil them down to half a dozen crucial tests which cover all the others, giving a tremendous saving of time and money.

However, the usefulness of ACLS was reduced by not having an efficient

*Published by Intelligent Terminals Ltd, 15 Canal St, Jericho, Oxford, OX2 6BH

database. All the data had to be specially entered. With ACLS interfaced to Superfile, the power of the rule finder can be applied to data whose collection has been greatly simplified by the database manager.

ACLS deals in two kinds of data. There are the 'attributes' – things that one thinks might be relevant to a rule; in the leprosy database, these might be size of village, average number of people per hut, distance to nearest fresh water, number of dogs. (It would not handle the names of plants, so the initial 'b' rule would not be found.) There is a second sort of data, the 'classification', i.e. the outcome that we want the rule to predict; in the leprosy example it is the incidence of leprosy in a particular village.

The user of ACLS-Superfile is presented with the screen form through which the data is entered and asks ACLS to look at certain fields and to form a rule to predict the entries in other fields. For instance, in a system to be used in a hospital intensive care unit to predict the outcome of heart attacks, the nurses might enter data about each patient on this screen form:

Patient [	]	Age [	A	]
Weight [	A	]	Height [	A	]
Blood pressure [	A	]	Pulse rate [	A	]
Lived/died [	C	]			

The user wants ACLS to look at the fields marked 'A' (for attribute) and to find a rule to predict the entry in the 'Lived/died' field – marked 'C' (for classification). ACLS will run and will produce a rule that might look like this (no claims are made for medical accuracy):

age
   ‹40:weight
     ›18:died
     ‹=18:lived
   ›=40:blood pressure
     ›120:died
     ‹=120:pulse rate
       ›100:died
       ‹=100:lived

This means: in order to predict whether a patient will live or die, first look at his age. If less than 40, look at his weight. If it is over 18 stone he will die, if less he will live. If his age is over 40 look at his blood pressure. If greater than 120 he will die. If less look at his pulse rate: if that is greater than 100 he will die, if less he will live.

ACLS runs reasonably quickly. It correlates each the value of each attribute in each example against the range of that attribute found in the examples to find fixed-value break points with a bearing on the classification field. It gives an answer fast, but it will miss rules based on more than one variable.

Very often rules depend on the relationship of one variable to several others in the same Record, rather than to fixed values.

One approach was BEAGLE, a program written by Richard Forsyth at the North London Polytechnic (see Forsyth, 1981). It produced rules in the following way. It was provided with a set of operators (greater than, less than, equality, plus, minus, divide, multiply etc.) which it could apply to the fields of the Records of a flat file database. It could make up rules and modify them at random. Each time it did this, it would test the prediction of the new rule against the classification field(s). If the rule performed better than others, it would be kept and a copy modified, again at random. If not, it would be erased.

Forsyth tested BEAGLE on a file of 100 heart attack patients. Some 16 measurements were made on each patient as he or she was admitted to Intensive Care – and the outcome of each case was noted. BEAGLE went through 500 generations of rules and came up with one that was 81% accurate. It said that if mean arterial pressure in (mm of mercury) is greater than or equal to urinary output (in ml/hr) subtracted from 61, the patient should survive; otherwise the patient is likely to die. This is a sort of test that no statistician would carry out because it compares values in different units. When Forsyth mentioned it to the doctors they initially said 'Rubbish!', and later, 'Well, maybe...' , because it is well known that the blood pressure of heart attack patients drops and their urination increases when their lives are sinking.

However, even this scheme will not fit all real-life problems. Imagine a database of share prices. Each Record consists of the price variations of a single share over some time scale. Now a rule finder that purports to predict share prices (which would be a profitable thing to own) would probably have to look at the prices of *all* shares at each date, because what we are interested in is the difference between our share and the general market index. Of course, we can side-step this problem in this case by including the market index in the database, but one can imagine situations in which things were not so simple. The value of railway shares, for instance, might be inversely correlated with the value of those for airlines.

Using the terminology of fields and Records, one might tentatively group intelligent databases into three classes:

(1) Those that look at the values of individual fields.
(2) Those that compare the values of fields in the same Record together.
(3) Those that compare the values of fields in different Records.

7.1 The problems of information

The human brain has an unrivalled ability to deduce 'rules' from random data. See, for example, the pseudo-sciences of astrology or phrenology. Since by definition, we do not know in advance what rules are hidden within our database, we do not know that there actually are any rules there, or if there, what sort of rules they might be. Any rule the computer can find can only be deduced from information available to it. This will often create difficulties which a human could easily resolve. For instance, a machine might puzzle for ever without discovering why sales of fur coats were poor in Africa. It might work for a long time to discover that the dates of invoices in a business in New York showed a periodicity modulo 7 – that is, that they were not issued on Saturdays and Sundays.

The database may conceal more complicated rules than the rule finder can extract – possibly because they draw on information not in the database. For instance, (assuming that leprosy and antimony are connected) it is hardly likely that so obvious a clue as an initial 'b' will signal plants that indicate the presence of antimony in the ground. It is more likely that this information would only appear if a second database of plants and their preferred trace elements was integrated with the test system. This would of course have to be run on a relational database manager and would produce a gigantic overhead as the rule finder tested out all sorts of other hypotheses about zinc, sulphur, cadmium etc. And one must imagine that there was no particular reason to use the trace element auxiliary database. The key to the problem might have lain in the victim's astrological sign, and one would need a database of the Houses and their birthdates. Or databases of political leanings – being a clue to the victims' tribal ancestry and therefore their genetic make-up.

Even supposing that databases of this sort of ancillary information were available on line, no conceivable processor could look through them fast enough to arrive at insights the brain does (occasionally) in a flash. Probably we shall soon see intelligent databases integrated with expert systems so that a human supervisor can tell the rule finding process not to bother about Saturday and Sunday when it comes to invoices; or alternatively, that it

Human thought often relies on the illuminating flash of lightning: the computer has to plod its way mechanically through mountains of data. Scientists disagree on whether a computer will ever be able to 'think' in the true sense.

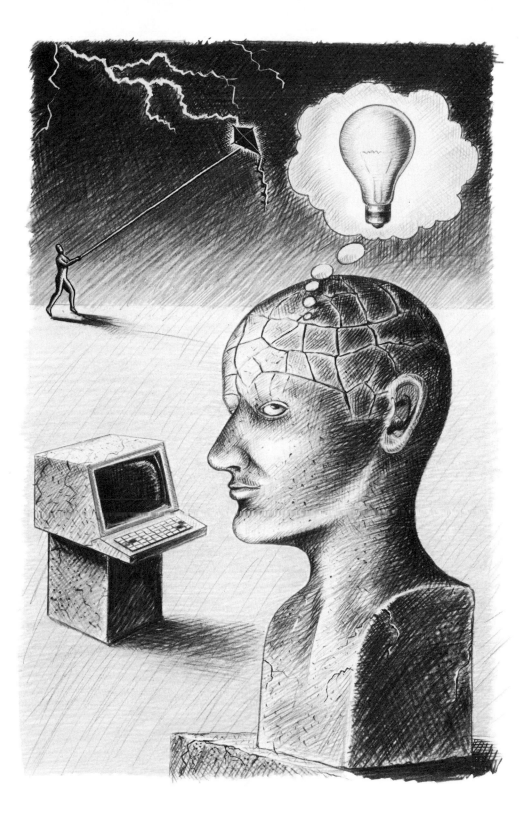

might be worth considering plant colours when investigating disease in the Sahara.

The range of possible information to be considered before a rule is found may be vast. So far there is absolutely no chance that any computer systems even in contemplation could possibly do the job. And this is presumably why good researchers are held in high esteem.

The brain's ability to store and access rapidly vast amounts of very ill-defined data presents an enormous hurdle to much effort in the AI field. What we call 'intelligence' in humans is often sloppy database retrieval on keys that should logically have no bearing on the subject. Often too, the retrieval is very roundabout, through what we would call a number of relational databases. The brain's ability to make flying leaps through these jungles of data is extraordinary. As one knows perfectly well by introspection, very few problems are solved by accessing vast numbers of irrelevant records until one finds one that is relevant. The insight either comes or it does not. So the failure of an intelligent database to produce a rule cannot be evidence that there are no rules to be found. Another big problem with an intelligent database is that people may believe what it says. Human affairs are so variable, it would foolish to assume that any rule deduced from a database at one moment will automatically apply to the same sort of data later on. The user of the intelligent database must cultivate a certain cynicism. An intelligent database that was 80% successful in predicting hopeless heart attack cases on admission could soon improve its success rate to 100%. Those cases for whom the computer foresaw an unfortunate outcome would have the sheet pulled over their heads by the attentive staff. They would immediately become ex-patients, demonstrating the accuracy of the rule.

Although a medical computer might look very authoritative and reliable it must be remembered that its rules will, for a long time, be based on a minute fraction of the tens of thousands of cases that medical training takes into account when young doctors are taught the elements of their trade. In any application we must remember that the computer is only an aid to human thought. It is, intellectually, a hewer of wood and a drawer of water. It has no ideas of its own and is lamentably prone to error. Still, if one takes it for what it is, it can be quite a useful little moron.

REFERENCES

Date, C.J. (1981) *An Introduction to Database Systems,* Addison Wesley, Reading, Mass.

Forsyth, R, (1981) BEAGLE: A Darwinian approach to pattern recognition, *Kybernetes,* **10,** 159-166.

Knuth, D. (1973) *The Art of Computer Programming,* vol. 3, Sorting and searching, Addison Wesley, Reading, Mass.

Laurie, P. (1983) *The Joy of Computers,* Hutchinson and Little/Brown, London/New York.

INDEX

68000 processor, 26

Accuracy, 122
ACLS, 130
Aeronautical charts, 77
AI, 127
Airline booking system, 24
Algorithms to do hashing, 49
Analogue concept learning system, 130
Apple
  Lisa, 22
  Macintosh, 22
Arabic, 13
Archiving, 125
Artificial intelligence, 127
ASCII, 13
Attributes (ACLS), 131
Audio cassettes, 91

BASIC, 104
Baud rate, 21
Bayesian logic, 130
BEAGLE, 132
BIOS, 35
Bits, 13
Book-keeping programs, 115
Book market, 116
Brain, 135
Branch (B-tree index), 54
Buffer, 15, 51
Bugs, 35
  and fixing them, 36
Byte, 13, 45, 76
Byte-rot; 38

Calculations, 101
Calculus, relational, 87
Cars of 1910, 7
Catholic church, 125
Census, 120
Checksum, 29
Chinese, 13

Classification (ACLS), 131
Clearance level, 63
COM 1, 21
Communication, 29
Computer, 9
Computer speech, 25
Console, 16
CP/M, 14
CP/M 80, 15
CP/M 86, 15, 117
Crashes and backups, 37

'D', 102
Data
  and disks, 11
  checking, 60
  distribution, 116
  list checking, 62
  range checking, 62
  sources and costs, 113
  updating, 97
Data protection, 114, 124
Data Protection Act, 63
Database, 9, 14, 39
  administrator, 110
  hierarchical, 60, 92, 93
  logical, 82
  multifile, 82
  pre-filled, 119
  relational, 60, 87
  searching the, 66
  three-dimensional, 107
  tree structured, 93
Database management, 9
  theory of, 7
Database manager, 39
Database system, 9
Datasolve's World Reporter, 117
Date, 110
Dates, 62
Day number, 62
DBA, 110

DBASE II, 101
Deadly embrace, 28
De-duplication, 89
Dental records, 76
/dev/lp, 21
Dewey decimal system, 48
Dictionary look-up, 60
Disk, 31, 32
　address, 48
　accessing, 12
　and data, 11
　double density, 32
　floppy, 11
　format, standard, 117
　hard, 11, 33
　laser, 33, 68
　memory, 10
　quad density 32
　read/write head, 50

Editor, 123
Electro-magnet, 11
Electronic mailbox, 118
Encryption, 63
Enquiry language, 39, 99
Error, 124
Expert system, 128
　disasters on oil rigs, 128
Expertease, 130

Field, 10, 42, 60
　key, 35
File, 13, 14, 45
　flat, 82, 92
　logical, 82
File server, 26
Filing cabinet, intelligent, 40
Fixed record system, 41
FMS-80, 102
Forms, 59
　generator, 60
Forsyth, Richard, 132
Front end, 59
Fuzzy matching, 66

Garbage collection, 70
Gazetteer, 77

Graph, 81
　plotters, 16
Graphics, 79

Hashing, 44, 47
Heart attack patients, 132
Heretical books, 125
History, obsolescence of, 125

IBM Personal Computer, 117
Idris, 15
Ikon, 22
Incredible Jack, The, 79
Index, 35, 70
　B-tree, 51
　file, 50
　minor, 47
　serial, 50
　size of, 47
Indexed Sequential Access Method, 54
Indexing, 45, 42
　of running text, 55
Intelligent database, 127
Interpreter, 36
ISAM, 54
Items, 10

Japanese, 13
Join, 88, 105, 108
Joystick, 22
Julian date, 62

Key field, 43
Key word, 56, 69
Keyboard, 16, 25
Knuth, Donald, 8, 49, 55, 67, 91

LAN, 26
Language compiler, 36
Leap years, 62
Lexis, 117
Links, 88
Local area network, 26
Loops, 101
Lotus 1 2 3, 79
LST, 21

Magnetic tape, 91
Magnetic medium, 32
Magnetism, 11
Mailing lists, 115
Mainframe, 26, 98
Maps, 77
Memory, virtual, 28
Michie, Professor Donald, 130
Micro-fiche, 31
Microwriter, 22
Mince, 79
Modem, 29, 119
Mouse, 22
MS-DOS, 14, 15, 117
Multi-processor, 26
Multi-tasking, 26
Multi-user, 26, 115

Network, 95
Nixon, Richard, 47
Node, 54
   leaf, 54

Operating system, 14
Overflow values, 49

Packet switched network, 30, 119
Page headers, 72
Paper, 31
Parallel file, 42
Parity, 21
Passwords, 63
Peripherals, 16, 22
Photofit pictures, 76
Physical safety, 63
Picture databases, 76
Picture field, 76
Pie chart, 81
Pixels, 76
Pointer, 43, 48
Port, 21
   serial and parallel, 21
Porting, software, 36
Printer, 16
   characteristics, 19
Programming around the database, 72
   in Superfile, 103

languages, 101
Project, 89
Prolog, 110
Proportional spacing, 19
Protection level, 63
Publisher, 123

RAM, 10, 16, 28, 31, 51, 58, 103
Read–write head, 11
Record, 10, 14, 59, 64, 82
   adding to existing, 44
   altering or erasing, 28
   deleting, 70
   fixed length, 60
   linked, 82
   list of qualities in a, 68
   locking, 28
   orphaned, 88
   that change shape, 45
   variable length, 74
   virtual, 28, 88
Reference books, 69
Relational database enquiry, 111
Report, 70
Report generator, 39, 70
Report line, 72
Reuters, 117

Schemas and data dictionaries, 110
Screen, 16
   touch sensitive, 24
Screen forms, 39, 70
   generator, 108
Search
   Boolean, 69
   many to many, 92
   phonetic, 66
   relational, 87
   serial, 46
Sectors, 12
Security, 63, 121, 125
Selection, 57
Sets, 88
Signature, electronic equivalents to, 122
Sirius, 32
Software, cost of, 37
Software maintenance, 36

Sorting, 57
    pack of cards, 57
Southdata, 8
Speed, 16, 64
Spread sheet, 41, 113
Spread sheet packages, 77
State secrets, 125
Stop bits, 21
Sub-total, 72
Superfile, 8, 44, 66, 70, 82, 84, 91
Support, 36
Synonyms, 57
Synthetic, 88
System manager, 63
System, telephone, 29

T-Maker, 79
Tables, 70
Tags, 44
Test and jump, 101
Text, 60
Text databases, 73

Text word, 11
Thesaurus, 57
Tidying, 70
Total, 72
Tracks, 12
Tree, 54

UK census, 120
Unique common item, 84
Unix, 15, 38

Values, 10
Variables, 101
VDU (visual display unit), 16, 26
Verification, 51, 62

Winchester, 33, 58, 68
Windows, 95
Word processing, 39, 113
    windowed, 108

Xenix, 15